To See Each Other's Good

Dorothy Yoder Nyce, Editor

Laurel Voran, Artist

Published by:
Dorothy Yoder Nyce
1603 S. 15th St.
Goshen, IN 46526

Library of Congress
Catalog Card No. 96-92276

ISBN 1-57579-016-5

Computer-generated typeset by:
Wordsworth
702 NE 24th Street
Newton Kansas

Printed in United States of America

PINE HILL PRESS, INC.
Freeman, S. Dak. 57029

Jo Esther Kniss

Friend of many in India
Gracious hostess of North Americans in India
Focus of the lead article

Acknowledgments

The editor wishes to acknowledge:

●A gift of $700 from the Frank H. Epp Memorial Fund, Ontario, Canada, to provide a small honoraria to contributors and to make some copies of *To See Each Other's Good* available to non North American women or organizations. The annual Fund provides financial assistance to projects that reflect concerns of the late Dr. Epp, a historian and church leader.

●Permission from the Council of International Ministries (representing Mennonite, Brethren in Christ, and affiliated overseas ministries) to edit and print the paper "Hopes and Struggles of the Church in South Asia," presented at the CIM meeting November 28-29, 1989.

●Two photos sent by Byrdalene Wyse of women from Argentina, included with the Mattie Marie Mast article.

Preface

To see each other's good calls readers and writers to pay attention to details, attitudes, feelings, and patterns. Each individual brings personal experience—its limits and breadth—to another's story. Writers about a person note unique features. Each narrative then reflects on the narrator as well as the subject. Another observer might highlight similar or quite different aspects of the same person, incident, or cultural dimension.

Each other's in the title suggests interplay between people. Exchange preceded and shaped each account here. Friendship, whether short or long-term, has occurred. Readers might look in these stories for the key qualities of friendship: "intimacy, admission of vulnerability, and openness of loving gesture" that Carolyn G. Heilbrun identifies in *Writing a Woman's Life.*

Good can be either adjective or noun; here it serves as the latter. Terms that characterize good also might describe or name an object, or function as a verb. Virtue, integrity, honor, worth, and genuine illustrate this. A woman might complete deeds that contribute to society or inspire others. Because she is worthful, she might prompt others to do their best. The intent here is not to elevate some at the expense of others but to intentionally name some so that the reader will recall others. Stories serve as models; individuals written about become mentors.

Various influences led me to gather stories. I knew that we learn through story whether conveyed by sermon, letter, conversation, or written account. I am a teacher, writer, and preacher as well as a student, reader, and listener. Other women have influenced my "becoming" in each of these roles. I also served eight years as a board member with Mennonite Board of Missions and observed several of this volume's writers in their international location. Further, when Esther Vogt died, the shortness of the MBM account of her forty years in India alarmed me; she deserved more recognition. I vowed to spread, not bury, wisdom like hers; to extend the voices of women became a sense of duty.

Encounters with women in India have enriched my life, nudging me to evaluate my western worldview. The teacher in me wishes to share new stories, values, metaphors, and beliefs about ways to be women. Rebecca S. Chopp expands on this in a *Memphis Seminary Journal* article titled, "Writing Women's Lives." Learning to know about both cultural differences and common truth can enlarge views and foster respect.

Initially, I invited three groups of women to submit stories. They included national women I knew who were in diverse countries, North American friends currently living in other global settings, and those earlier in an international setting but now living in North America. A number of stories from all three appear here. A second volume will include twenty other stories. Writers were invited to tell about a national woman or some distinct experience for women in a given country.

As women, our collective task includes honesty in revealing our own stories and helping others to tell theirs. Then we listen with care, setting aside stereotyping which restricts our hearing. Our theology might limit whether we receive another's truth. "Being church" and following the radical Jesus may be quite political in some locations. Our task also entails study of further sources, for these stories do not answer all questions we need to process to become world-sensitive Christians.

I dedicate this book to a friend, Esther Kniss; her story appears first here. Esther's story about her friend follows. After several brief accounts of specific women, writers combine anecdotes of given women with information about organizations. Following contributions from four non-North American women (two writing about a country other than their own), more stories of individual women appear. The book concludes with several stories that utilize the personal letter form. Nonetheless, each story stands alone.

To See Each Other's Good is an attempt to publicize esteem felt for the women named here. By inviting writers, I expressed my value of them for who they are and what they have experienced. Writing about the good in another is one way to say, "Thanks for how you have mentored me."

Another friend, Laurel Voran, expresses her "good" or gift through art work created for this collection.

Most authors of these stories claim Mennonite heritage. More than

half of the worldwide Mennonite family live on continents other than
Europe and North America; to exchange about culture and society becomes
increasingly important. Representatives will gather for Mennonite World
Conference in Calcutta, India, in January of 1997. Books like this might
scatter with them on leaving.

Several writers reflect insight from diverse Christian groups. We live
in the midst of the World Council of Churches '88-'98 Ecumenical Decade:
Churches in Solidarity with Women. I wish I could have included more
stories from writers who believe in God through a living religion other than
Christian. Many writers included here have learned from such women of
faith.

An article "Beginning Where We Are" by Kathryn Anderson, Susan
Armitage, Dana Jack and Judith Wittner appears in the 1990 *Feminist
Research Methods*. The article suggests: Include less well-known as well as
distinct lives, activities, and feelings. Reflect on how the woman's experience
fits into a wider context. Ask, "Does what she did, or how she felt about it,
differ from what was expected of her?" The goal is to help stories emerge.

With each story in this collection, I provide a statement of what to
"anticipate." Ideas stem from the resources noted in this introduction. Not
intended to limit what you see, they might cause you to observe more.

Let each story unfold. And reflect, on completing each, about
further questions you might ask the woman met in each article. Think about
how your story does or does not intersect with hers. The book you may put
down, but let significant ideas or feelings linger to prod you "to see each
other's good."

Dorothy Yoder Nyce
Goshen, Indiana

Table of Contents

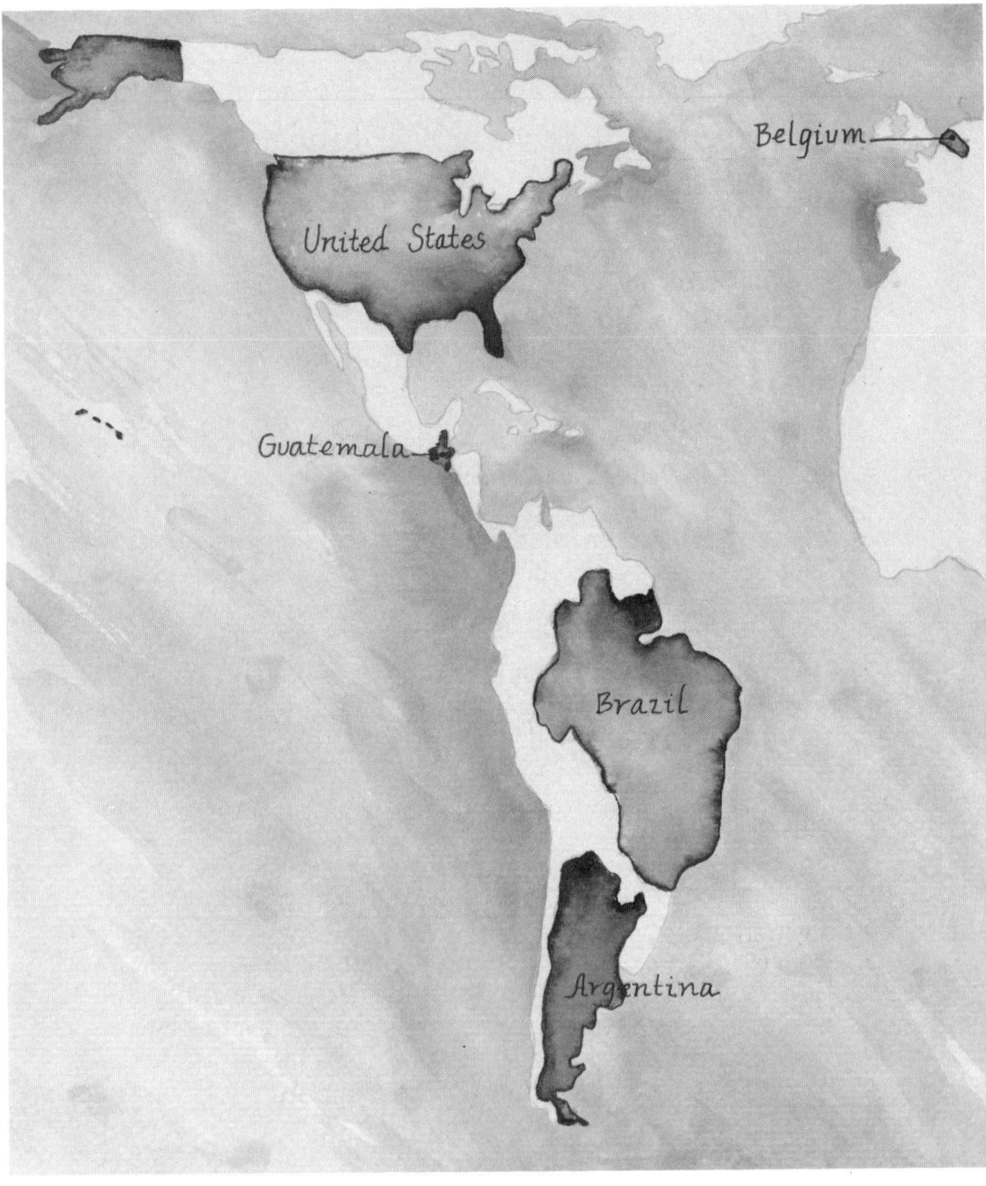
Belgium
United States
Guatemala
Brazil
Argentina

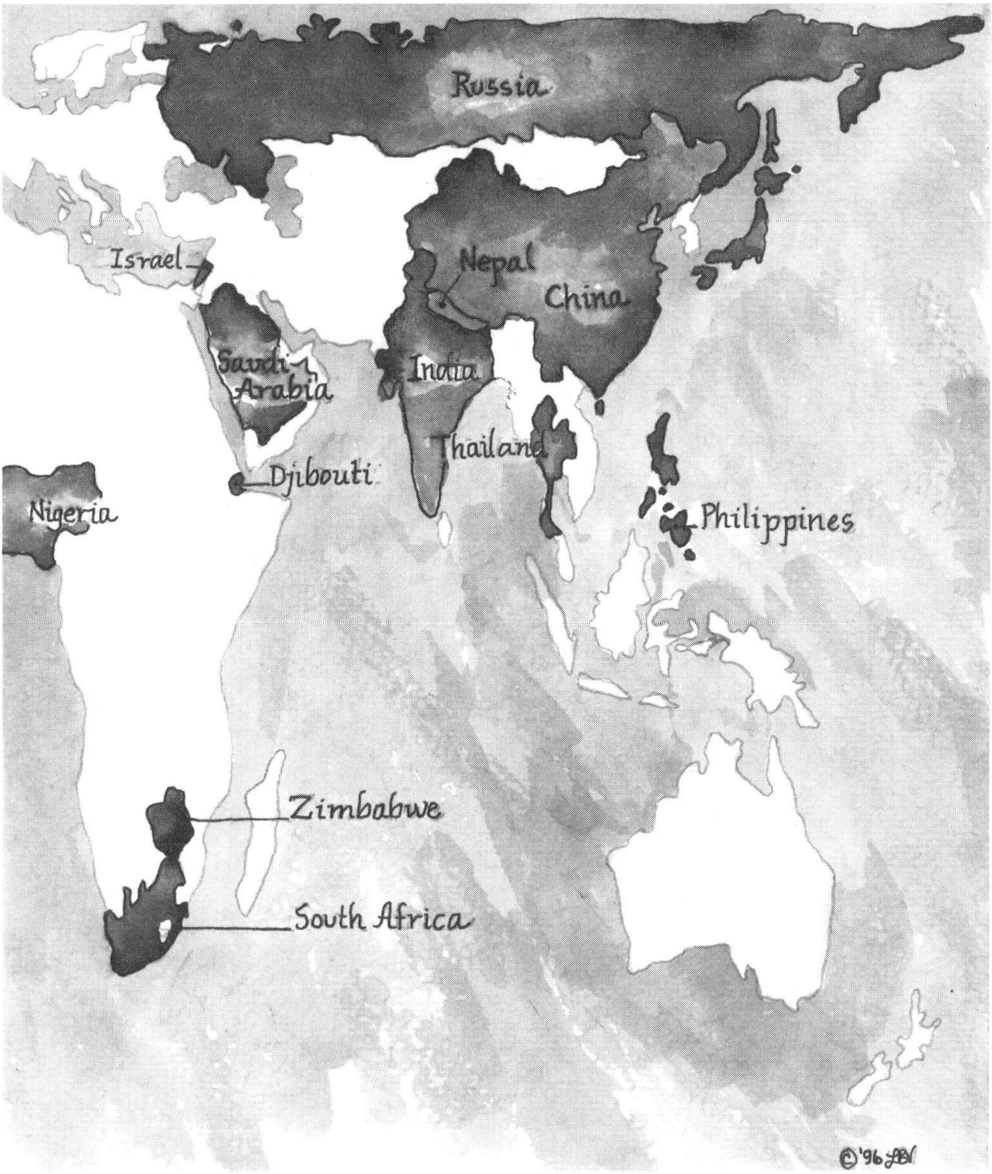

Russia
Israel
Nepal
China
Saudi Arabia
India
Thailand
Djibouti
Nigeria
Philippines
Zimbabwe
South Africa
©'96 LBV

1

For Such a Time as This
Esther Kniss

Dorothy Yoder Nyce[*]

> *Anticipate how details of Esther Kniss's actions convey what she values. Not passive, she causes things to happen. This account draws on an interview with Esther in the Kniss home in Bihar, India, in March 1993, and numerous previous visits.*

In December 1962, I left the foothills of the Himalayas with my husband, John, for two months on our first winter vacation from teaching at Woodstock School in India. We high-stepped into the battered bus to head down the hill. Hairpin curves seemed as wild as they had to us on our trip up in July.

In Dehra Dun, we boarded the overnight train to Delhi, to spend the first of thirty nights in sleeping bags. Traveling third class, we spread out our sleeping bags on top bunks (boards less than a meter from the ceiling, and held in place by sturdy chains), while strangers spread out their bedrolls on the benches below us.

Several more train, bus, and truck rides awaited us before we met

---

[*]Dorothy Yoder Nyce is currently a DMin student, writer, and teacher. She is the editor of this book.

Esther and Paul Kniss for the first time. Enroute, in a deserted train yard, a delay to connect bogies (train cars) seemed endless. With no lights on in the train car, I watched shadows from a distant, dim, pole light play games in our space. There in a stillness penetrated by a train whistle even more distant, I pondered the meaning of "family," as I wondered in what ways Esther and I would resonate. Her name prompted further questions.

Do you at times wonder why parents choose a particular name for a child? Some children "wear" that which is given them with ease; others resent the choice. A few legally change it. Times change too. And the significance linked to a name may shift, depending on the time.

In ancient Israel, a name's meaning was thought to shape character. Old Testament Esther's name may stem from the Persian *sitareh* meaning star or be a late name form of the Babylonian goddess Ishtar.

So why might a Mast couple from Oley, Pennsylvania, have decided to name a daughter Esther? Perhaps they recalled another Esther—from a family tree, from a favorite childhood story or paperdoll, or from ancient Israel's account. Esther Mast later became Esther Kniss, a missionary for more than forty years in India, beginning in 1950. Having the same first name hardly guarantees common experience. But characteristics true for Israel's Esther and Esther Kniss do shine—each a star in her own sphere.

Each Esther lived in a culture other than hers by birth. She was an outsider. In order to cross cultures, each weighed distinct trademarks of her heritage and chose to alter certain details. Scriptural Esther likely ate foods less than kosher; she kept secret a key dimension of her identity—religion. Due to government surveillance patterns, the Knisses at times lived with uncertainty. So, each Esther took risks. Threat and opportunity intersected "for such a time as this" (Esther 4:14).

Both Esthers earned favor among those with whom they lived. Women of prayer, each remained faithful to her religion while living among people of another faith. From each, a keen observer learns of the overruling power of Providence. Each engaged in self-reflection too. Not arrogant, each knew her strengths and Source of strength.

Not wishing to stretch the comparison too far, each did, however, affect what others read. Aware of one written decree with potential to destroy Israel, Esther sought the king's attention to reverse that with another. People of his 127 provinces read the revised version. So also, countering limited knowledge, Esther Kniss helped many in the greater Ranchi, Bihar, region to gain access to books—for faith or classroom. Each knew the power of word dispersed.

I trust that readers truly interested in people's cross-cultural experience will welcome details. Moved to think beyond our own frame of reference, we will imagine. We will try to comprehend that in India, for instance, the image can be more important than word. Readers will, hopefully, feel or see parts of Esther Kniss's varied landscape in order to credit her routine but timely life.

See a squatting potter whose small, bare foot controls the speed of his wheel. His deft fingers shape a vessel from moist, earth-red clay. Or, imagine an array of barefoot school boys in khaki shorts. The school bag of each drapes from a shoulder or dangles loosely from his waist. At dusk a herd of cows saunters by; their wooden bell clappers gently strike with each sideways shift.

Open yourself to the bustle of a bus stand. Cluttered, the area thrives with tied bundles, with passengers destined for a dusty ride. Battered buses wait; their horns invite the late to hop aboard.

Then, upon arrival at Knisses, watch Esther's household worker. His ready smile shows pleasure in serving the curry meal he just prepared. Even his name, Emmanuel—"God with us"—assures Esther and Paul of Divine presence.

For just a moment, I cannot help but refer to another Esther I knew in Bihar. Esther Vogt taught us informally about animism. In a religion with a strong sense of the existence of spirits and demons, natural objects *live*, she noted. Without judgment, Esther explained rituals of engagement and wedding, as we watched the events progress. She walked with us across barren fields to clusters of earthen homes. Women stopped their work of creating mats or baskets from local reeds, to visit. An infant nursed from what seemed a depleted breast. Mutual respect occurred between conversant Esther and shy villagers. Nuances and body language picked up where our meagre facility with the language failed.

While John and I were young teachers at Woodstock School, we spent parts of three winter vacations in Bihar state. In that 1962 Christmas vacation, our friendship with Knisses began. What about their hospitality drew us back three times? Genuine welcome, conversation, and appreciation set the pace. A friendly dog added spirit—the recent dachshund Tiny passed everyone headed up the stairs. Comfortable, even a haven, described the Kniss home, regardless of address.

I remember one Christmas day. Knisses and we attended a forenoon wedding reception at a village home. Seeing the quantity of foot-long plant roots being peeled for their meal lingers vividly in my memory. We visited several other homes; hosts always served tea. I clearly remember that black pepper was substituted for sugar. How that burning sensation left its mark, seemingly from throat to sternum! But Paul likely failed to notice; his spread of red pepper on a fried egg disqualified the category mild. When we returned to their pleasant home in Chandwa, a tasty vegetable soup left no need for turkey. Even their living room carpet invited us to lie down to watch the kerosene lamp shadows mark time with taped carols.

I asked several people to highlight their memories of Esther Kniss. Several began with a series of adjectives. Lynette Beachy Bauman said, "gracious hostess, confident, and one with distinct organizational skills." Her sister Cheryl Beachy Paulovich added, "Quiet, constant presence. Plus, you felt accepted with her." For five years the Beachy family and Knisses lived on the same property.

Wilbert Shenk, Mennonite Board of Missions administrator during half of Esther's forty-three years in India, noted the following about Esther: "gracious, cordial in relating, evident competence, efficient, and reliable. You knew you were in good hands with her; you could depend on her assessment of a situation."

Coworkers Laura and Dale Schumm stressed Esther's "sensitivity to what was going on around her, to people, and to relationships." They added, "She was a strong mission team member. Her calm confidence shaped herself, the group, and the process."

Esther is an authentic friend. Lynette characterizes her friendship as warmth. While for the Beachy children Esther was always called Auntie, for Lynette's daughter Bethany, Esther became Grandma. In 1986 John and my daughters experienced her genuine interest, too. She helped them, as North American teenagers, to learn about a segment of rural life in Bihar. They gained insight into privilege, rather than taking so much for granted.

Esther always received guests with grace. Whenever we arrived, with or without our children, just off a memorable train ride in the '60s or from an Indian Airlines swoop into Ranchi in the '90s, she always offered water on arrival—to drink or to refresh our body's skin.

Mealtimes followed. Memorable details include: the tinkle of the brass bell, the tea pot in its cozy, a seasonal floral centerpiece, place mats of the handwoven *Ikkadu* type from Chingleput District, dinnerware with a simple blue design on white. Devotions, as regular as breakfast, kept all abreast of Mennonite involvements worldwide, in addition to the day's scripture. Conversation reflected on dimensions of the day, ahead or nearly complete, and much more.

I can see Esther at the table end: light brown hair pulled back from her narrow face framed with glasses, a ready smile. Humor complemented most meals. Esther could enjoy any anecdote, whether or not she had heard it before from Paul. When she laughed vigorously, her hand might cover her mouth.

Laughter and friendship with Indian nationals proved central for Esther too. She watched Emmanuel's children grow into adulthood; most recently living space with his family was separated only by a small hall. Esther took interest in each woman and young girl gathered for church. With Mrs. Davis a special bond grew. (See Esther's article about Mrs. Davis in this volume.) For each other, they were "like family." Inspired by the other, each could depend on the other to be with her in pain, physical or emotional. A recent note to me from Mrs. Davis confirmed, "We greatly miss Paul and Esther's presence in Ranchi now."

Mutually reliable, Mrs. Davis and Esther shared common interests in organizations, people, and beauty. Coworkers with the YWCA, the Rose Society, or Red Cross efforts, they met often with committees. They confidently met the public, forming useful contacts and gaining solid rapport. Prime Minister Indira Gandhi attended a rose show with which they were involved. Esther and Mrs. Davis were pleased to judge and give prizes for unique varieties.

From flowers to faith, I find in this friendship a most worthy quality. Each extended the other "religious space." Knowledgeable about the broader church, Mrs. Davis participated less actively than Esther. With Christianity claimed by less than three percent of India's population, people of different denominations must learn from and understand each other's programs. In a city like Ranchi, opportunity for Mrs. Davis and Esther to form an interfaith group for friendship and exchange about faith, also illustrates the theme "for such a time as this."

Esther's relationship with Mrs. Sharma, her Hindu landlady, enriched both. Their differences of faith did not hinder mutual respect.

What could be a more profound proof of friendship than Mrs. Sharma's daily gifts of food after Esther was bedfast with severe back pain? What reflects more the spirit of foot washing than her repeated back and leg rubs? Therein was faith expressed!

That reminds me of another act of love, that Esther wished to share involving her husband, Paul. A couple of Indian women found themselves stranded in a swelling river. After watching Paul Kniss retrieve them from this life-threatening experience, a young boy chose to follow the One who motivated that selfless act. Many have been the opportunities for Knisses to both extend and receive Divine love in the multireligious land that is India.

Early in Esther's sojourn in Bihar, she walked with "Bible women" to visit women in villages. Some knew only a local dialect; Esther's knowledge of Hindi had its limits. These national women, assigned by the church, told Bible stories and taught simple hygiene and nutrition. They were key instruments "for such a time" for conveying religious and cultural insight. They also taught Esther to be guarded about issues of health—of dirt, human waste, or spittle.

Sexual matters rarely entered conversation. But Esther learned cultural meanings linked to a woman who maintained eye contact with a male stranger or even waved to a male acquaintance. She came to deal also with smart remarks or intentional touch from young boys who likely enjoy being risqué. Such "eve teasing" increased generally over the years within the country.

Risks of survival restrict population control measures. "As long as women are not valued, there will be more children," Esther said. That she and Paul did not bear children sometimes prompted Indians to respond to them with apology.

While fifty percent of the region's women were illiterate in the early '50s, now seventy-five percent can read. When Esther first taught women's classes, she created flannelgraph depictions of ten simple but significant Bible stories. She discovered common, yet profound, ways to contextualize the creation story. Because of cultural animist beliefs, people took keen interest in stories of Jesus' driving out spirits. Cultural dimensions also gave Esther new insight into the miracle of Jesus as a healer. Frequent requests for Paul's medical supplies or common sense prompted this further. More fundamental than medicine or faith issues, however, Knisses learned—as did Lutheran and Disciples workers with area people of animist heritage—the importance of winning peoples' trust.

Esther achieved such trust partly through Bihar Mennonite Mission (BMM) tours. During the winter months of October through February, for stints of a week to ten days, she lived with one remote village group or another. One woman she met had had a vision of "someone who would come to save." What multiple facets of being saved from or to meant, Esther did not elaborate. But, to share God's love and "let God" live among people in God's own way describes one aspect of grace. Constant grace, like the rice and *dal* the women shared.

Esther came to better understand the hardship conditions of rural Bihar too. People struggled to survive because of debt, for example. Some individuals or families inherited debt from their parents and never existed outside of it. Such bondage became practical grist for Esther's sharing about ancient Israel in bondage.

Regions of Bihar have struggled more than once from drought. Relief agencies then mobilized Food-for-Work projects, paying hundreds in food staples for work done. Projects included digging out ponds to hold the hoped-for monsoon rains. Rows of human conveyor belts walked the ridges carrying load after load of earth on hip or head.

Hardship also prompts people to beg. In India, anyone with a white face can become a target for an expected handout. Response in public calls for tact—someone begged from me inside a church. To greet a beggar at the door of her home, requesting rupees or food, was rarely simple for Esther. What might a meeting "for such a time" mean? She said she "longed to be able to do more" but also remained gracious in the midst of poverty.

But the Knisses had options. They could find renewal through short stints away from problems. When the beauty of nature beckoned, they went trekking on occasion in India's northern mountains. While sightseeing remained limited, they traveled some in India to attend meetings of Boards on which either served, such as Emmanuel Hospital Association.

By 1955 public talk against foreign missionaries had surfaced where the Knisses ministered. Work among tribals was suspect. Suspicion receded or increased at various times during the Knisses' forty years in India. To understand it would require insight into political realities before and since India's Independence in '47. It would call, further, for background into interreligious currents and the interplay of cultural facets. This article cannot tackle all of that. I only wish to caution against simplistic or naive judgments or faulty bias. Knisses continued to live with government surveillance. Cultural views about financial linkage to a United States agency affected this. Their faith that God sustains "for such a time" upheld them.

Different faith-related activities developed. At times a Bible school was held with church workers and their wives. Families lived on the mission compound while taking classes on food, sewing, and music. Youth camps and Vacation Bible School also nurtured the young in faith.

Safe but spartan hostels provided housing, work, and ties of friendship for students in schools some distance from their village. Esther explained the local hostel arrangement. Young girls from distant villages—their long, black hair neatly braided—lived together in a single room and attended a nearby school. Because of this, more Christian girls were able to pursue education.

Esther and Paul were active with church groups—sometimes two or three per Sunday—at scattered locations. While visiting with people before or after worship, they supported and further instilled basics of faith. To see leaders emerge reinforced sacred ministry.

From their Chandwa home-*cum*-office, Knisses began to sell books. Believers with some reading skill longed to learn from the increased number of books published. Students enrolled in all standard levels needed texts and notebooks. These, combined with greeting cards, wall pictures and writing supplies, proved to be a worthy enterprise. A small business, Good Books, was begun. From this, they "grew into book store work," Esther said. In the early '70s, they helped form the Good Books Educational Trust, which assumed ownership of the business.

For nearly thirty years, Knisses gave concerted time to this Ranchi bookstore and four branch stores. Esther's skills were invaluable. Laura and Dale Schumm noted her key competence: "She was primarily a manager-teacher. She understood and explained both bookkeeping and finances—so that others understood. She had a most unique place in and commendable way of relating to the Indian male culture."

Esther encouraged and instilled confidence. She took personal interest in all the workers as friends: women and men, sales people, those who filled mail orders, department managers. Schumms added, "She gave responsibility and expected accountability in return." She modeled meeting the public. Her comment, "I had such interesting conversations with customers" was likely how many of them felt about it, too.

High standards of relating and of conducting business set the tone. These prompted legitimate pride in a task done well. They involved honesty and respect—for self and other. A management committee enhanced stability and steady progress. The result was longevity of the business.

John and I were privileged to attend the March 31, 1993, staff "function"—a catered dinner—to complete a fiscal year and to honor workers, including one employed for twenty-five years.

Esther and Paul's sustained partnership has also been significant. Wilbert Shenk "thinks of the two together, although each had distinct spheres of work. Their enjoyment of India was genuinely shared."

Whereas Paul had grown up in India, Esther adapted to the culture as an adult. Yet both needed formal training to read and write Hindi upon arrival in March 1950. The Beachy sisters expressed different views about Esther's following Paul. One commented, "She adjusted to the importance of her husband's past, yet did not hide in his glory." The other "wonders what all was involved for Esther, to commit herself to another's likely preference of place to be." Esther alone knows this. Whether a wife chooses, or is culturally conditioned to comply with, a husband's choice of work or location affects internalized feelings for many women.

Both Beachy sisters have fond childhood memories of having lived near Knisses. "We did a lot together; like extended family, we were all a part of everything," Cheryl recalls, adding: "Esther taught me how to knit." Lynette remembers listening to records at Knisses. She said, "And I was impressed with how well Esther could drive in Indian traffic. How she, as a woman, related to business men and church leaders also struck me." She concluded, "It would not be India, without them."

Esther told about several cultural changes during her years in India. In the early decades, "I wore primarily cotton saris," she said. (To note cotton is to contrast it with the distinctive silk saris notable there.) Cotton is common among rural women. Chuckling, Esther recalled discovering "that foreigners take longer steps. The sari can feel more limiting, for stride as well as doing certain tasks."

Now more women wear the trend-setting, two-piece *shalwar* chemise. In the '60s we called this a Punjabi outfit, since it was worn most commonly by women from the Punjab region. Usually of cotton, the loose-fitting (except at the ankle) pant piece is tied with a draw string at the waist. The more dress-like, knee length top varies in sleeve length. Either fairly plain or more decorated, some color of the top matches the pant. Whereas a loose, eight-inch by five-foot strip of cloth formerly was crossed in front and draped over each shoulder, this now might drape over only the left shoulder. That resembles the one end of a sari drape. Esther wears either the sari or *shalwar* chemise with grace. She also wears western skirts and blouses, especially since moving to Ranchi. Young Indian rural girls choose among these options, while city teenagers often add jeans or slacks.

Another noticeable change for Knisses centers in electricity. Its gradual increase corresponds with more household appliances being available. Earlier Knisses depended on kerosene or petrol (gas) pressure lamps. Today's electrical supply has reached even most rural areas. A term common to city experience is "load-shedding." With this, a region of a city can expect to be without current for certain hours of the day or night. "Sure enough, it's seven o'clock," Esther commented as she recalled where to locate a torch (flashlight) to find the nearest lamp. Off for an hour, then on an hour before off the next, the cycle of energy fluctuates, and people adapt.

As surely as Esther quoted the Proverbs text—"Her Works Bring Her Praise"—to title her article about Mrs. Davis, so the phrase describes Esther's dedicated energy and vision in India. We saw another sign of this during our 1993 visit.

Although Esther had been diagnosed with giant-cell, or temporal arteritis, of which a side effect of the medication was osteoporosis, she wanted to "conquer" a computer. After regular periods of rest for compressed fractures of some vertebrae, and properly braced, she spent blocks of time learning computer details from John. She planned, in turn, to teach Good Books staff, updating and making more efficient the store's management. What a gift of determination "for such a time!"

That determination reminds me of Esther of ancient Israel who changed from a hesitant orphan to a decisive female. Esther's relative challenged her to enter the king's contest, and later his presence. Though uninvited and therefore countering royal rule on the latter occasion, thus taking personal risk, for such a strategic time of survival for her people, she could not remain silent.

Comparison between the ancient story and the experience of Esther Kniss are not parallel, of course. But I am intrigued by how they intersect, by how qualities of character overlap. Each challenged some established ideas of what was expected of her. For the story of each, understanding the wider context remains essential. While neither birthed children, each "mothered" people in convincing ways. Although a foreigner, each woman cooperated in God's Cause to bring Truth.

Truth of another sort dawned when Knisses realized that, due to Esther's increased problems with compression fractures, they would return to the States earlier than expected. Their final month's whirl of activity meant handing over responsibility, sorting and packing, and saying "Good-byes." "For such a time" as that, words fail to express distinct feelings.

At one time Knisses had applied for Indian citizenship. Not granted, they faced the tough uprooting stage prior to transplanting. How often Esther had watched farmers do that to rice. During future springs, she will recall how women prepare the soil to plant. She will think of the weeding and cutting, the improved seed, the dung-enriched soil.

Other details will flash into Esther's memory: the roadside sellers of toothbrush bundles (neem tree twigs); the "*Yishu Sahai*" ("Jesus Be Your Helper") greeting with each person before and after worship services; the morning devotions with Chandwa household helpers under the banyan tree whose branches grow shoots that take root and become new trunks.

May the Esthers of faith know that they have provided strong roots that will, for such times as needed, grow into solid trunks. And may *To See Each Other's Good* honor Esther Kniss, its "star."

2

Her Works Bring Her Praise
Alleyama Eapen Davis

Esther Kniss[*]

> *Anticipate what Mrs. Davis actually did, rather than defer to presumptions about women's tasks. Discover what she values and why, and observe an assertive, courageous style.*

"Auntie! Auntie! *Namaskar* (greetings)!" A middle-aged business man called out, his hands respectfully clasped together in greeting. "Do you remember me?"

Mrs. Davis and I were about to enter a grain shop in a busy market area when this man came out of the crowded street to greet her.

"Yes, Narayan, how are you? What are you doing in Ranchi?" Mrs. Davis asked. She returned the gesture of respect—a statement of honor for God within the one greeted. She remembered when Narayan Babu—an alternately violent and then depressed patient—had arrived at her Kishore Nursing Home years ago. After a month in the Home,

---

[*]Esther Kniss lived in India 43 years before retiring to Virginia in 1993. As a Mennonite Board of Missions worker, her tasks were church-related and women-related, through many genuine friendships, Good Books, and organizations like the YWCA. She is the subject of the first article in this collection.

Narayan had left in good cheer, grateful for the effective and kind treatment he had received.

Before proceeding into the shop, Mrs. Davis talked a few moments with Narayan. As he went smiling on his way, she addressed the shopkeeper.

"Gopal Babu, *Namaskar!*" She greeted him, her palms graciously brought together again. "This is Mrs. Kniss with me. We have come to you for help. I need five hundred rupees from you for our YWCA (Young Women's Christian Association) building project."

"Ah, Mrs. Davis, of course! How can I refuse you? Gopal Babu sent a helper to bring tea for us while he went to his cash box for the money.

"No, please, Gopalji (*ji* being an ending that denotes respect), we just had tea. Some other time." This was the fifth visit of the afternoon for us. We had already been served tea at two of the places.

Rarely does one person make such an impact on a community or city as Alleyama Eapen Davis has on the people around Ranchi. (This Indian city in the state of Bihar, northwest of Calcutta, is home for nearly a million people.) Even more remarkable, this "outsider" arrived in Ranchi with little skill in the Hindi language. Before long, however, she established her credentials and became an important citizen—a "Mother" or "Auntie" to many people.

Alleyama Eapen was born in Kerala, the South Indian state where the literacy rate is higher than many places in India. Unemployment is also high. Therefore, many people from Kerala go north or abroad for jobs. Alleyama came to Ranchi in 1944. As a young nurse, her first job was in a government mental hospital. In 1948 she competed for an All-India scholarship. The winner, she went to London for three and a half years of in-service training in Maudsley Hospital.

On her return to India, Alleyama responded to an advertisement for a qualified "Anglo-Indian or European" mental health nurse for the post of Superintendent of Nursing. When she went for her interview, she was told that she was not eligible because she was Indian.

She demanded, "But you have to take me. I am fully qualified, having done well at such a prestigious place as Maudsley. If you turn me down because I'm an Indian, I'll take this matter to court." Her British interviewers must have been either pleased with her spunkiness or fearful of her threat. They hired her.

The Medical Superintendent at the "European Mental Hospital" was Major Davis, a British doctor who was born in India to missionary parents. His father was a medical doctor, his mother a teacher. Dr. Davis had served in the British Army a few years before going to India to head this government hospital. He and Alleyama got along so well together that they decided to marry. After seven years of co-directing the medical and nursing services of the hospital, they started their own nursing home for patients. Major Davis continued as part-time consultant and teacher in the hospital.

The new Kishore Nursing Home was first built on rented property. Within eight years, 180 patients were receiving care in the wards which were often separate buildings. The Davises also bought a small farm and raised crops to help feed the patients. The reputation for low-cost, good care at Kishore drew people from great distances.

After eight years, Dr. and Mrs. Davis bought a tract of fifteen acres. They started building their own facilities—home, wards and offices, staff quarters, dairy barn, and poultry house. They installed pumps and laid out gardens. They developed the new facilities to accommodate up to 300 patients. Mrs. Davis did most of the farm management, plus much of the nursing home management, while her husband was occupied with his research and practice.

Two daughters and a son were born to them during these years. Major Davis received awards from both Queen Elizabeth and the President of India for his distinguished service.

In 1980, while on a visit-*cum*-study break in the United States with his son Charles, Major Davis died of a heart attack. While the two daughters were in medical school, Mrs. Davis and Charles carried on the work of the Kishore Nursing Home and the Davis Institute of Neuro-Psychiatry. Daughters Rachel and Lizzie finished their medical training also. While doing postgraduate studies in psychiatry, they joined the medical staff of the Nursing Home.

Even now, in her seventies, Mrs. Davis is always busy. A person may find her registering patients, peeling potatoes, supervising the garden work—which some patients use for occupational therapy—taking care of the cows, or cutting limes to make pickle for chutney, a common Indian relish. When she sits to visit with a friend, her hands are not idle either.

She may be cutting vegetables or tying twists of colored paper on string for Christmas decorations.

Or Mrs. Davis might be away from Kishore—attending a meeting of the Rose Society or the YWCA. An active member of the Rotary Club for many years, she was the first woman in India to be elected president of her club.

She was named "Farmer of the Year" a few years ago for her record production of rice per acre. Between scattered lime or papaya or banana trees, her garden has two or three kinds of vegetable plants in rows. With different kinds of plants in various stages of development, the land does not lie dormant.

The Nursing Home is known far and wide; it accommodates from 275 to 300 patients. As little as twenty-five rupees a day (less than a U.S. dollar) has been the minimal charge for inpatients. This covers medicines, nursing care, and food. Inpatients usually stay twenty-eight to thirty days. Forty to sixty outpatients attend the daily clinic. Rachel, Lizzie, and Lizzie's husband Miland—all qualified psychiatrists—work tirelessly along with the other doctors.

A documentary film was made of mental health institutions. Kishore Nursing Home was featured and recognized as an effective, low-cost mental health care center. The hub of all the activity is Alleyama Eapen Davis—"Auntie" or "Mother" to hundreds who found health through her diligent ministrations.

Indeed, "her works bring her praise" (Proverbs 31:31).

3

Pregnancy: A Linkage to Friendship in China

*Margaret Metzler**

> *Anticipate some hidden thoughts and feelings through honest exploring of a private realm. As Carolyn G. Heilbrun suggests in Writing a Woman's Life, intimacy, admission of vulnerability, and openness of loving gesture are essential qualities for friendship. Observe also how choices interact with cultural teachings.*

To create stories of friendship in China has limits because to form real friendships can be difficult. My contacts are primarily with students; the typical teacher-student relationship does not foster closeness. However, young people not yet conditioned to such reserve feel more free to explore, as the following accounts reveal.

Few women peers have been my friends in China. One reason for this is that they realize that they could be faulted later for forming close

---

*Margaret Metzler has lived twenty-seven years in the Orient: twelve years in VietNam, six in Hong Kong, and nine in China. She teaches English and serves as a pastor to China Educational Exchange workers, sponsored by Mennonite Central Committee. Mother of five children, she is a writer and volunteer hospital chaplain.

relationships with foreigners. When too friendly with us, they feel conspicuous or under suspicion.

I remember meeting one Christian woman who knew no English. At that time, I could speak little Chinese. By contrast, her husband was fluent with English and conversed easily. However, this woman knit me a beautiful, triangular scarf with an intricate design. I find friendship woven through those threads.

Miss M and Miss D*—During my first year in Sichuan Province, I enjoyed a particular three-person friendship with two younger women. Miss M was the Chinese secretary in the foreign language department of the university where my husband and I taught English. Miss D was an American woman who had come earlier to China to teach (and to escape the aftermath of a painful divorce). Here, she fell in love with a handsome, bright, young Chinese student.

Early in their marriage, Miss D became pregnant. For varied reasons, the couple decided the timing was not good to continue the pregnancy. She underwent an abortion, which left painful emotional scars. When she became pregnant about a year later, however, there was no doubt that they dearly wanted this baby.

Interestingly, Miss M became pregnant about the same time. Although these two women were already good friends, this common, special experience drew them close to each other. As a mother and grandmother, I became deeply involved with each of them as individuals. We shared many close, personal feelings over a period of several months.

Miss M's earlier inability to conceive had been somewhat unusual. During the first few months of the school term, she was sometimes absent from the office for a day, or a half-day. As she was the epitome of efficiency in a somewhat easy-going society, this seemed unusual. She then whispered to me, "I'm seeing special clinical experts at a downtown hospital who are trying to help me become pregnant."

I remember when she shared the details of her story. Her husband, stationed with the military in Tibet, had home leaves only for the yearly Spring Festival and perhaps one other time. I wondered if he received special permission for an extended leave while the experts

---

*Full names are not disclosed, to respect privacy.

helped them conceive.

Her family had pressured her for years to have The Child. In a society where only one child is officially permitted and where the task of continuing the family line is crucial, the family remains the prime unit of society. A young woman's key role is to conceive, to bear that child. Failure to do so sets a woman apart as strange, as other than normal. The society ostracizes her. Young wives who do not conceive suffer a great deal. Adoption therefore is uncommon, although some children do need homes.

When her first signs of pregnancy appeared, Miss M immediately was "not well." Her mother came from a distant place to oversee her care and activities. When her mother moved into the one-room home, her husband returned to his unit. She insisted that Miss M stay in bed and keep her knees close together, to prevent any chance of miscarriage. Although the weather was not cold, she was kept bundled up. Fortunately, morning sickness did not continue long; she was soon happily back at work, proudly pregnant.

Miss D, who was closely involved with her Chinese husband's family, told me of varied societal understandings about pregnancy. She shared the pain she felt when family members blamed her for the earlier abortion. She should have birthed the child and given it to a relative, they said. "It would have been so beautiful and bright, being of mixed races!"

In the privacy of our apartment, the expectant women shared in depth their experience of pregnancy. Then I left for extended vacation. By the time I returned in the fall, Miss D and her husband had moved to the United States. I hurried to Miss M's home; she was not there.

A neighbor led me to the next building where Miss M was living temporarily. She was obviously in her glory. When she had birthed a fine baby boy in mid-August, with her husband present from Tibet for the happy occasion, a colleague had offered the use of an empty apartment. After a few weeks, her husband returned to his unit.

Miss M moved back to her small home, filled with her books and personal possessions. The infant sleeps on one side of her bed, wrapped warmly in layers to avoid rolling off. Her husband's younger sister also lives there to assist with infant care. Miss M is on maternity leave until next term. I enjoy stopping at her home to hold her baby, hear her talk about his antics, and observe her pride.

For a long time, Miss M has dreamed of going to the United States. Before her pregnancy, she had contacted a number of institutions about options. But to have her child first was important; she could be more trusted to return. Married for eight years and now in her thirties add to the ideal timing. Having fulfilled her parents' dreams and societal expectations, she continues to secretly make her plans. In a matter-of-fact way, she expects to leave her small son in the care of others during two or more years of study abroad.

Miss S—I first learned to know Miss S when she was a Chinese teacher studying for one year at Goshen College in Indiana. Then a thirty-year-old with five years' teaching experience at a Chinese university, she traveled with us in the United States to see friends. Our friendship continues in China; she frequents our apartment to talk shop and to share hugs of greeting and farewell. Such demonstration of affection is not common in China. But she and other students seem to crave expressions of friendship.

Miss S has also described her and her husband's predicament about having The Child. Both parental families are pressuring them to conceive. But the couple is very happy without a child. They see the prospect of parenthood in terms of hard work, sacrifice, and giving up personal ambitions. Her husband has a good computer job through which he finds challenge and happiness.

Not happy teaching English here, Miss S dreams of returning to the United States to pursue a Master's degree. To get the necessary permission and make arrangements is not easy since she already studied abroad. However, as with many other determined young people, she is willing to go to extreme ends to meet her goal.

Having a child might help her to achieve her study dream. With a child remaining in China while she studied abroad, officials could expect her to return. But she thinks this is a poor reason for bearing a child. Besides, she and her husband do not "need" (even dread having) a child in order to feel fulfilled. This attitude, while rare in China, is growing among young couples. For it, they face family and social ridicule. Society maintains that the only normal family life is a threesome—father, mother, and child—with the grandparents hovering nearby.

I'm grateful to learn that cross-cultural friendship provides recurring occasion to blend openness and integrity with wisdom.

4

Thank You, Maria!

*Ada Schrock**

Anticipate attention to feelings, attitudes, values, and meanings.

Thank you, dear Maria,
>   for sharing with us so deeply.
>   What an inspiration and challenge you brought to us!

You came to D.C. from your home in Nigeria,
>   via New York City where you'd stopped with a friend,
>   to undergo surgery on your face,
>   to correct a problem from an accident years ago.

You introduced yourself during your first tea-time as
>   the mother of five children and
>   a teaching nurse-midwife.

---

*Ada Schrock is a former secondary and elementary school teacher from Pennsylvania. During retirement, Ada was a volunteer at the Washington, D.C. International Guest House maintained by Allegheny Conference of the Mennonite Church to provide short-term, inexpensive housing for international visitors to the District of Columbia. While on the IGH staff, Ada met Maria to whom she wrote this free verse. More recently, an accident has left Ada with minimal sight.

In later encounters your vibrant faith in God came through
　　　　loud and clear as you spoke of the ways
　　　　in which God has led and blessed you,
　　　　through the years, through thick and thin.

As you shared,
　　　　you often had conversations with God,
　　　　repeating the expression, "My God," as natural address—
　　　　just as you'd speak to one of us—
　　　　a far cry from the secular use of that phrase.

We sensed your vital affinity with God.
　　　　And as you spoke of your work,
　　　　you shared your strong conviction
　　　　that to serve humankind is so much more important
　　　　than to earn excessive dollars.

And then, Saturday afternoon, I took the call
　　　　from a church just down the street,
　　　　where you'd gone for an African cultural event.
　　　　I learned that you'd been mugged,
　　　　right after you'd left the church;
　　　　that you'd returned there to call the police.

"How could this have happened,"
        I kept asking myself,
        "in this quiet, residential section,
        in broad daylight!"

When you came back to IGH, you were still visibly shaken.
        Your glasses were broken,
        but at least your face had not been injured.
        Despite your physical struggle
        plus verbal appeal for your vital papers,
        the thief had taken your bag plus all its contents—
                including a large amount of cash
                which you had failed to put into a safe place
                after a trip to the bank the day before.

We listened to your anguished account
        of the dreadful incident,
        mended your glasses temporarily,
        loaned you some cash,
        and simply loved you. . .

If only you had removed that cash from your bag,
        if only you had not taken that shortcut
                through the alley,
        if only the thief had given you your papers,
        if only. . .
        But those were *our* "if onlys";
        you were just so grateful
                that your face had not been injured.
        You were not angry at God for "letting this happen."
        You asked none of the normal questions,
                like "Why do bad things happen to good people?"

On Monday, before going to the Nigerian Embassy
        to see what kind of help they could proffer,
        you asked us to think with you in prayer.
        We joined hands and prayed, each one in turn,
        for wisdom in your efforts
                to make amends for this shocking misfortune.

And after we had talked with God,
    you started singing softly
    "Abraham's blessings are mine,
    Abraham's blessings are mine,
    Believe it or not,
    Abraham's blessings are mine."

I could hardly believe my ears, and yet,
    having heard your earlier witness, your beliefs,
    why should I have known surprise?

So, thank you, dear Maria,
    for living out a genuine faith in God,
    for calling me to deepen my own trust.
    For, I have no doubt
        that as you later left for Saudi Arabia,
        you could address, with integrity,
        the prevailing enmity between Christians and Moslems—
    a further, more subtle, encounter with "saving face."

5

Finding the Sacred in Nepal
Janaki Devi, Rashmira Maharjan

Miriam Krantz[*]

> *Anticipate reading about cultural or relational features free
> of judgment that might stifle your seeing a woman's
> strength. Situate each individual within her social setting to
> realize how tradition can cause her to be vulnerable in the
> world.*

Pilgrimage Toward Peace and Acceptance—One morning during the communion service, my glance paused with the oldest member of the church, 88-year-old Janaki Devi. Her expressive face was full of devotion as she played the cymbals and sang: ". . . for me He died, for me He was buried, for me He rose from the dead; I am His and He is mine." My eyes became moist as I joined her and the others to claim Jesus' constant presence and to remember what his life and death accomplished in our behalf.

Janaki Devi was raised as a devout Hindu. Childless and widowed at a young age, she went on long pilgrimages all over India to find peace. She hoped to gain merit to help overcome socialized disgrace of widows.

---

[*]Miriam Krantz is Nutrition Consultant to UMN (United Mission to Nepal). Her creation of "super flour" porridge has benefited many. Four times a Nepali colleague has moved into Miriam's former job, since she first went to Nepal in 1963.

In Nepal, she spent twelve years going from one Hindu holy place to another. By then she was very poor and alone.

One day a few years ago, as she attempted to cross a busy road, a vehicle almost ran her down. Almost. Someone reached out to pull her to the side of the road. That someone was a church member. Their conversation by the roadside led to Janaki Devi's asking to attend worship. She had known nothing about Christians. Before long, she claimed faith in Christ and became a member of the church.

Every Saturday she boards a bus near her home in a town on the edge of Kathmandu Valley to travel to the heart of the capital city, Kathmandu. From there, she takes another bus across the river. She depends on her sturdy, beautifully-carved cane to pick her way up the uneven, dirt path to the church. There she removes her sandals. Leaning on her cane, she moves down the aisle to her favorite place near the front. Someone helps her sit down on the floor and places her cane beside her. She bows her snow-white head in prayer and worship.

Janaki Devi has found peace and acceptance in Jesus and with his followers. Only one short pilgrimage remains for Janaki Devi to take—not a pilgrimage to counter disgrace, but a joyous climax to faith. Meanwhile, she inspires us all, reminding us of God's grace, transforming power, and faithfulness.

Abundant Commitment, Abundant Life—With sparkling eyes, Rashmira Maharjan warmly welcomes each member of the Abundant Life Committee to join her in prayer.

What is her background? Rashmira was born forty years ago in an orthodox Hindu-*cum*-Buddhist town. She had nine brothers and sisters; now only three live. She was told that five died of smallpox and malnutrition during childhood. When she was six or seven years old, Rashmira started to attend the only Sunday School in her town. She remembers her childhood ambition to teach children.

Then her mother became ill and spent two months in the mission hospital. She was asked why her children did not attend school. A doctor taught Rashmira to read in the two months her mother was hospitalized. She offered to take Rashmira to her own country for school. But the mother said, "No, she can learn here."

After her mother was discharged from the hospital, Rashmira

was put directly into Class Two at school. Later, she skipped another class. After Class Six, she could not attend school regularly.

When Rashmira was fifteen, her mother died. Although part of a joint family in which different generations live together, Rashmira had the difficult task of caring for her father, two brothers and a sister. That same year she began working as an interpreter at the hospital. Rashmira chuckles as she recounts one incident during that half year. The doctor said to her, "Please bring the scissors." Rashmira rushed off and brought back the nursing "sister" instead!

Rashmira next received on-the-job training for the maternal child health (MCH) clinic and general ward nursing. With money earned, she was able to send both brothers and her sister to school.

When she was sixteen, Rashmira expressed full faith in Jesus Christ. Severe persecution followed. When her sister died of fever, Rashmira was blamed. On one occasion her father restricted her to his own room for three days without food or water. He tore up her Bible.

He took the pages to his shop, to use to wrap spices and other items for customers. Rashmira felt great joy that the Word of God was thereby so widely dispersed.

Meanwhile, she searched her father's room for something to read. Finding the Gospel of John, she read this over and over. She prayed and sang songs. When a hospital friend stopped to ask how many days she needed to stay in the room, her father replied, "I don't know; she's happy in there."

Once her father swung her around by her thick, long braid. He beat her until her older brother begged him to stop. Neighbors crowded into the room to spit on her. But even throughout this difficult time Rashmira felt at peace. After such an experience, everyone knew that Rashmira had become a Christian. No one would eat or drink anything she touched. Rashmira recalled, with a twinkle in her eye, that after that she no longer had to fetch all the water for the family. Later, her father apologized for mistreating her.

Rashmira's father became very sick. Before he died, he asked to be told about Jesus. He requested that the door be left open so that others could also hear. Once he revived after losing consciousness. During that final week, he shared his faith with his entire family and others. Just before dying, he spoke of Jesus and prayed. Rashmira, then eighteen, chose to be baptised.

Rashmira worked hard; she paid off half of her father's hospital bill. When her brothers became established with jobs, and after she had worked as a nurse for a year in another hospital, she trained as an auxiliary nurse midwife (ANM). In that role, she served in a community health program for three years before and eight months after her marriage.

Christian friends arranged her marriage when she was twenty-six years old. Her non-Christian brother agreed to the marriage and the young man, but refused to attend the wedding. After his own marriage, he stopped talking to her. Her younger brother remains in contact. Rashmira's great love for her brothers continues.

Rashmira's first baby arrived prematurely, weighing only 1.9 kilograms (4.2 pounds) The newborn had problems retaining food. Although the doctor initially felt hopeless, the infant left the hospital after two months. She thrived on her mother's milk and, after five months, supplementary feedings of "super flour" porridge. The latter she continued to enjoy for breakfast until age five. Now a bright thirteen-year-old, she has an equally bright eleven-year-old brother.

Rashmira, after local training as a health assistant (HA), held a very responsible position at the district hospital for eight years. Whenever she went into villages, she was moved by seeing great spiritual and physical needs. Led to resign her secure hospital job, she began full-time ministry.

Her vision led her to form an Abundant Life Committee in February 1991. Churches in four of the five regions of Nepal have welcomed Abundant Life seminars, which offer both spiritual and physical health dimensions. At the first one for pastors, representatives attended from sixteen out of twenty-three congregations in the area. Non-Christians also request such health training seminars. Always generous and practical with her skills and gifts, she expresses gratitude for how God has led step-by-step in her life, family, and ministry.

Rashmira encourages Christian women with Jesus' words: "Until the end of the world I am with you." She adds, "Many problems come for women. But when confident, we can do what is needed. Encouraged, we know Jesus' presence."

[A close friend of the author suggests that after reading these accounts, readers may wish to pray for the person named.]

6

Daughters of
Abraham and Sarah

Nancy Martin[*]

> *Anticipate the need to be sensitive to women's perceptions*
> *of their choices or responses. Are we free to evaluate and*
> *question our own culture's values or way to order life prior*
> *to judging another's specific setting?*

The women of Israel and the occupied territories, both Israeli and
Palestinian, are women of strength and courage. Israel has named
everyone born in this land "Sabra." This is the name of a cactus fruit that
is prickly on the outside and tender and sweet on the inside. This often
characterizes the women, as well as men.

To be woman within this context is to be defined primarily in
terms of societal expectation. Woman's function or role is to give birth.
Mothers are highly valued and given respect and honor. To have
community status, a married woman must have a son. The children of
Israel, Arab and Jew alike, are generally cared for responsibly. They are
the focus of family life.

Israel's laws protect job security for women on maternity leave.

---

[*]Nancy Martin recently completed the role of director of Nursing
Education for the Nazareth Hospital School of Nursing. Along with other
degrees, she holds an Ed.D in administration and C.S. (clinical
specialist). She and her husband are parents of two adult children.

All who give birth in Israel have their hospital costs paid. Further, the state pays for a layette for each newborn baby. Labor laws give time allowances for breast-feeding and sick days for women employees who need to stay home to care for sick children.

In the Arab community single women feel tremendous family and societal pressure to marry. Once married, a woman's goal is to become pregnant as soon as possible. Infertility is greatly feared. Fertility clinics are sought out after six months of marriage without conception. After giving birth to a first-born son, parents gladly give up their own names and become Abu (father) and Im (mother), followed by the name of the son.

The family value system greatly affects health priorities. The following vignettes, from the Arab community, tell of family health experiences with which staff of the Nazareth Hospital became partners. In Nazareth, hometown to Jesus the Healer, the healing tradition continues.

Ihm Ahmend and Granny—The time was spring of the third year of the *intifada*, the Palestinian uprising against Israeli military occupation. A young married woman who lived in the northern section of the West Bank gave birth to her first-born child, a son Ahmed. The parents of Ahmed are Moslems and first cousins. They thanked God for breaking into their very difficult lives during the *intifada* with the joyous gift of a son. Rounds of congratulations were heard—good wishes with Arabic words of blessing "May God keep him."

From the very beginning, feeding problems weakened this infant. Nearby family members at first thought this was due to Im Ahmed's inexperience. They shared with her their years of accumulated wisdom. The baby's problem persisted, however, and by the age of six weeks, Ahmed's birth weight of 3,700 grams had dropped to 2,350.

The young parents brought their child across the "green line," which separated Israel from the occupied territories, for care at the Nazareth Hospital. Prior to this, Ahmed had been hospitalized frequently at Nablus and Tulkarem, located in the northern part of the West Bank, suffering from both pneumonia and poor feeding. He had undergone nose and throat surgery in an attempt to correct the feeding problem. The admission diagnosis at Nazareth was severe malnutrition due to neuromuscular swallowing difficulty.

Im Ahmed was frustrated because breast-feeding was impossible; Ahmed could not suck well. He also refused a bottle. Finally the doctors and nurses wanted Im Ahmed to feed him through a feeding tube inserted down the back of his throat into the stomach. She did not like this unnatural process in which she could not hold him. However, since this was the only way Ahmed could avoid vomiting or aspirating, she continued. Reward followed in weight gain. Three weeks later, at the age of nine weeks, his weight had returned to 3,440 grams.

Late summer found the paternal grandmother staying with the child for another long hospitalization. A grandmother is expected to care for children of her sons. Hospital staff endured the grandmother's demands. Her towering presence—in long-flowing traditional dress and headcover—hovered near, protecting the often febrile child. He was further restrained by intravenous antibiotic lines and feeding tubes.

Finally, the staff declared Ahmed ready to go home. Granny refused. She intuitively knew that danger lurked. Just then the nurses noted food coming once again from his nose. Diagnosis showed quick fatigue of face and neck muscles. In spite of the latest treatment available, the outcome could prove to be counterproductive.

When the Gulf War broke out in the Middle East. Im and Abu Ahmed, like all other inhabitants of the region, either fled with their families or went on to a survival foothold. The Scud missiles crossed overhead, but Ahmed and his parents survived the war. Two weeks after his first birthday, Ahmed began vomiting with each feeding; he developed a fever. Once again he was admitted to the Nazareth Hospital, accompanied by his grandmother. Now the child had scabies also.

Ahmed's father had a very difficult time crossing the "green line" border. Security concerns and measures had been heightened and tightened. The border patrol often accused Abu of lying. They mistreated him when he asked to cross into Israel to see his sick son. Viewed as less of a security risk than Abu Ahmed, the grandmother crossed with greater ease.

Ahmed, although the size of a typical one-year-old, was very weak and lethargic. His condition deteriorated. Finally, in the presence of his grandmother, Ahmed died in the intensive care unit. With all the tubes and lines removed, the granny held and cradled the dead child's body as she wept and rocked out her grief.

Abu Ahmed was called hours before, to warn him of the

impending death. But he could not come, for he had just taken his wife to another hospital. That very day, she gave birth to a second son.

Omaima—Spring in Galilee is beautiful—clear blue skies and fields ablaze with myriads of wild flowers. In the spring of 1991, just after the Gulf War, such outdoor beauty prompted a family of six—parents and four healthy children—from a small village just north of Nazareth, to enjoy a day-long picnic.. Having been cooped up in sealed rooms with gas masks, the family's need for air and space was understandable.

Omaima, age six-and-a-half, and her family chose the beach at Ein Gev on the east side of the Sea of Galilee—forty-five minutes by car from Nazareth—for their picnic site. After the meal, Omaima was the first to run to the car, parked by the lake, to change into her swimsuit. She did not return. What happened to her after that only their imaginations could "explain."

Military and civil patrols launched a massive, but unsuccessful, search. Ten days later a fisherman found Omaima. She was sun-tanned and her skin showed signs of exposure. She reported having slept in the fields after playing alone during the day. She denies contact with, abuse from, or attack by anyone. Although very thin, exhausted, and covered with scratches over her lower arms and legs, she showed no signs of sexual molestation. She remained calm amid everyone else's excitement. She showed no signs of psychological disturbance.

Omaima was admitted to the hospital for examination. She became the focus of a lot of media and public attention. Doctors were amazed to discover only mild dehydration. Asked what she ate and drank while alone, she denied doing either. The nursing staff concluded that she likely drank from the lake and ate anything she could find.

Her grateful parents stayed by her bedside. Four days later she went home—her scratches cleaned and healed through intravenous antibiotics. She was three kilograms (6.6 pounds) heavier than when she was admitted to the hospital. No one returned a week later for the scheduled follow-up visit. The lost lamb had been found and restored.

Subheeye—Organs for transplant are not available in this part of the Middle East. Religious beliefs concerning the body prevent donation of organs by those brain-dead from accident or disease. So Egypt has become a marketplace for kidneys. Egyptians and other African men who need money have exchanged one of their kidneys for funds. Such capital might be needed to build a house or to make a person eligible for marriage. Those who make such deals conceal their donation of an organ, even from their own families.

Subheeye, a 61-year-old, married woman of Nazareth, needed renal dialysis three times each week because of kidney failure. She would come to the hospital and be hooked up to a kidney machine for about five hours while her blood was washed of its waste products. Her failing kidneys were not her only health problems. She was an insulin-dependent diabetic, with poor eyesight from complications of diabetes. She was from the Christian Arab community.

Subheeye's husband was a man of considerable financial means. He decided they should go to Egypt to explore buying a kidney so that Subheeye could be freed of being dialyzed by machine. He tells how he needed to bargain a hard deal with the donor. They both met the donor, a young Ethiopian man, before striking a deal. At an Egyptian hospital, the donor's harvested kidney was transplanted to Subheeye. The donor returned to Ethiopia with his money, and Subheeye the recipient went back to Israel with her acquired kidney.

Ten months after the transplant, Subheeye was still sick and required frequent visits to doctors and hospitals. While Subheeye was free of the need for dialysis, her new kidney did not work well because of systemic pathology in the new host.

Final Examples—Staff of the Nazareth hospital hear many current stories or discover windows into how destinies of people are determined by circumstances they could not control. One Russian Jewish immigrant came to the out-patient clinic with signs of stress. She and her husband had been in an immigration depot in Europe. Fearing a resurgence of pogroms, they were fleeing from possible persecution or organized massacre. She thought they were waiting in a line of people going to the United States. When the line was divided with only two people in front of them, those remaining were told that the quota was filled. They and those behind them were sent to Israel.

Or, consider another approach to destiny. Two women nurses concluded a busy day with an errand to another department. Outside the maternity department, they passed a newborn baby, wrapped in a crocheted blue and white blanket, lying in the center of a trolley. At the end of the trolley sat a nonchalant young man whose legs dangled over the edge. He seemed to look at everything but see nothing. One of the nurses commented that a woman would never leave a baby alone like that. Not after carrying an infant in utero for nine months and enduring the birth process.

Twenty minutes later they were proven wrong. Returning via the trolley, they found the new baby all alone and the young man nowhere in sight. Five meters away, on the other side of the corridor, sat two women. One of the nurses asked the women if the baby belonged to one of them. A prompt response was offered: "Do you want her? Please have her."

Clinically, this scenario is called dysfunctional bonding. It usually means that the mother's needs are not being met. She has nothing to give to the infant. The infant was a girl, disguised in a blue wrap intended for a son. Who will she become?

King Solomon watched the parade of life here too. He used Divine wisdom to determine which woman in the brothel was the true mother of a child (1 Kings 3:16 ff). Despite human schemes, God oversees. And surely, at times, God must weep over the daughters of Abraham and Sarah.

7

Poetic Silence

Gayle Gerber Koontz[*]

Anticipate exploring the meaning of varied forms of conflict. Allow the writer and the subject to choose which experiences and feelings are central. Listen and hear.

These five poems speak of different kinds of silences that I experienced in a militarily-contested area in the mountains of Negros, Philippines, in 1989. Military struggles continue.

With fifty other people, I entered a "no man's land" to investigate the report of a farmer's wife. She told of the murders two months before of three men and two boys (ages two and four) by five paramilitary men and three government soldiers. The men and boys were taken from their farms and killed because they were suspected of being revolutionary soldiers (or, in the case of the children, eventually-to-be soldiers).

Since this was identified as a likely human rights violation case, we accompanied a government health official to exhume the graves. Death certificates, needed for prosecution, could then be issued. We also wanted to secure an affidavit from an eyewitness who was arrested by the

---

[*]Gayle Gerber Koontz taught at Silliman Divinity School in the Philippines for two years in the late '80s. With a Ph.D., she is Professor of Theology at Associated Mennonite Biblical Seminaries, Elkhart, Indiana, having been Academic Dean and for one semester Interim President.

same men but who had escaped. (At the time, the witness still carried the slug in his back with which he was shot when running away.) He remained in hiding in the area.

We also took supplies to offer material and medical assistance to farm families of these remote areas who try to stay with their land. They have no other means of livelihood. They fear to come down to the town because others who have done so have been arrested, imprisoned, or killed as suspected revolutionaries or supporters of revolutionaries. Yet, they must constantly "hide" in the mountains also. They are subject to military operations by both government and revolutionary forces.

These farmers have difficulty growing much more than root crops which have limited nutritional value. Military and paramilitary men, as well as thieves, sometimes move in and harvest other crops just as they are getting ripe. Or they forcefully take pigs and other animals from the farmers for their own use. The children that we saw were beginning to show signs of malnutrition.

Because we had no guide who knew where land mines had been planted, we needed to follow a laborious route up and down mountains to reach the graves. We carried our food and water. I was grateful for clouds and rain.

On the second day near dark we found and exhumed the several-month-old graves, a sickening task. One of the men's skulls indicated that a bullet had entered from the back of his head at close range. Other evidence showed that legs had been broken. I saw the bones of the two

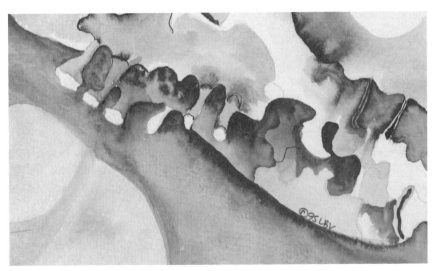

children and an adult, as they were removed from the earth below a mango tree at the top of a hill.

The following day we met the pregnant wife of this adult man, the mother of the two dead children. She told us her story in her native tongue without emotion: how the armed men had come and taken her husband, who was working in the field near their home with the other men, and then the children from the house, and left. Later they heard shots but, fearing to follow, did not go to find the bodies until the next day. The children had been disemboweled.

Another woman told us her story: how on her way down from the hills to market with two relatives, the three were stopped by paramilitary men. Their money was taken and they were thrown into a deep crevice. Her relatives—a man and a woman—died. This third person had used an umbrella a relative of hers had been carrying to pull her way up out of the rocks. That effort took three days. She had been afraid to tell any authorities about the incident.

After dark a small group of men, women, and children from that area met with us, crowded into a now-abandoned, two-room house. As is typical in Filipino company, we shared songs and stories. One of the farmers picked up the guitar and began softly to sing. His was a song of hope for freedom from these circumstances, to the tune of "Silent Night." Hearing that, the pregnant woman whose husband and children had been killed, who had so stoically told her story, began to weep. The others surrounded and held her.

That night, as we lay stretched out toe to toe, with no room to roll, I slept uneasily. Not so much because of lack of space, but because of the insecurity of the place. I thought, "They live with this day by night by day . . ."

On the way down we stopped by the farm where the men had been working in the fields when they were taken to be killed. The house was completely gone. I remember the thin, lined face of the fifty-year-old woman who had lived there and who had led our way to the graves. I remember her hands lifting, digging, and wrapping an orchid plant from the tree near her former front door—a gift to us of beauty and life. It was the poignant gift of a survivor—a woman of sorrow, a woman of strength.

No Man's Land

I

Climbing
there is no breath for words
only silent step
upon step
hands burning from cogon cuts
up and up.
Pungent lemon grass,
friendly roots,
rain streaming
from banana leaf to cup
host the way.
Hours later
I lean mud-tired
dripping
into a windbent hill.
Manang,
five years older
rice sack on head
toes spreading earth and rock
walks straight
to her husband's grave.

II

Silence
like white smoke from the rice pot fire
stings.
No cock stirs the dawn.
No firewood cracks, no child's cry.
Wind creeps up the mountain
and down
softly
like a barefoot farmer
hiding.
The stirring in her womb

brings no smile now
cut
from her man, two sons.
The silent night lingers
shredding
her tears.
Only the rain
soaking the mango tree
weeps.

III

Music warms the room
like hot sweet coffee.
Cigarette tips dance in the dark.
For a moment
laughter fills the pit
into which they had been thrown,
she alone
clinging to a ledge
three days in and upward
out of the silence.
The guitar holds us
lifting
releasing
the strings of our lives.
A match flares.
Song gifts
speak what cannot be spoken.
Outside
the moon weaves
silver grasses
soft questions
weaves a soul song
still.

IV

The rolled leaf wick
fades.

We lie back to back
side to side
knees curled,
shifting space for one more
one more.
Soft insect slaps, a child's protest
punctuate
half-sleep.
Cold seeps through floor cracks.
Restless
I strain at the silence.
Gunshots in the distance
or only night breaths
near?
The memory of an armed man's face
swathed bandit like
cap erasing eyes
intimidates
sleep.

                    V
Once brown hands reached
for boongon
tearing husks away
cradling fruit's tender tang,
reached for coconuts
slicing them wet
dripping from chin and hands,
scraping meat with carver's care,
child's delight.
Once brown hands poured water
splashing into clay pots,
forced the grinding stone,
tended orchid bursts,
fed the fire.

Now
fruit waits.

Mungo pods hang black in the field.
Dry corn
sags on the stalk.
One cup guards a fire-scarred post,
a lid
neighbors
a broken jar,
the silent grindstone
sinks
into the memory of a home.

Dumaguete City, Philippines
May 1989

8

From Lethargy to Leadership
Leonor Mendez

*Janet M. Brenneman**

> *Anticipate beginning where a woman is, and has been. She is the subject and authoritative speaker of her own experience. To be free to call into question some past patterns can expand one's belief about being a woman in the church.*

The ten-year-old Guatemalan girl sat at her school desk, her head in her hands. To concentrate on tasks was hard. Her hope lay in the five *centavo* coin stuck in her shoe, and in the specific instructions for getting to her own mother's house. Her stomach growled. On some other days, she had fainted from hunger and the exertion of early morning chores before going to school.

This morning her teacher had sent the little girl back to her father's house because her uniform was not clean. Her stepmother beat her unmercifully. Before returning to school, she was sent to the meat shop to buy meat for the dog. This was the opportunity for which the

---

*Janet M. Brenneman has been a good friend of Leonor for two decades. After ten plus years in community development and leadership training in Honduras through Eastern Mennonite Board of Missions, she directed the Bible Institute for three years. She currently is Director of the Basic Studies department of SEMILLA, the Latin American Anabaptist Seminary, in Guatemala City.

child had waited. She did not return home after school. With the five *centavo* coin, she boarded the designated bus and watched carefully to get off at the right street corner. She counted the houses and arrived safely at her mother's doorstep.

"In your minds you must be the same as Christ Jesus," the speaker said, quoting from the second chapter of Philippians. "We are asked to be his hands that heal and restore," she continued with a clear voice. "We are asked to be his feet that go where few choose to go. Not only asked to give our gifts, Jesus asks for our very lives. We are asked to give and receive forgiveness. We are asked to accompany the afflicted, to feel their pain." With such conviction Leonor Mendez preached at an evening mass session of Mennonite World Conference in Winnipeg, Canada, in July 1990.

The speaker was Guatemalan. Thirty years before, she was the child who had kept the five *centavo* coin within reach at all times. What transpired between these two incidents—to give the woman broad experience and compassion—is the focus of this story.

Leonor Mendez was born in 1949 in Guatemala City, the first of three daughters. She was four when her Christian parents separated. The youngest daughter was not yet born when Leonor and her sister went to live with their mother. After a year her father remarried. The new, eighteen-year-old bride stipulated a condition for marriage: the two older girls would live with them, so the father would not visit his former wife's house. He reclaimed them legally.

From the start, the girls suffered a gamut of daily punishments from their stepmother. Insecure as a mother, perhaps this was her way to exert authority.

"I never had a childhood," Leonor recalls. "I worked hard, sweeping and mopping the house and going to the store. I took care of my little sister. I washed our clothes and did the ironing. I don't remember playing, only working."

Leonor's father was also a hard worker. He gave inexpensive injections in the early morning, then worked for a pharmacist. Later, he had his own pharmacy. He ignored his wife's treatment of his daughters. "She would have said the punishments were your fault," he told Leonor years later; "you would have said they were her fault." To not decide between the two was easier for him.

Nevertheless, Leonor credits her father for her early concepts of God. "He would read to us at the table, and he came to our room at night to pray with us. He was a church deacon and elder; he directed some mission efforts. But he separated church life from the reality of daily life in our house. Between job and church, he was seldom home."

At school, Leonor's teacher showed concern for the little girl who often arrived dirty and hungry. She brought food for the child, to help her survive the morning. This she gave unnoticed, to avoid embarrassing Leonor in front of classmates.

One day at church the teacher noticed a little girl who resembled the listless Leonor. She told the child's mother that her daughter looked like a girl in her classroom.

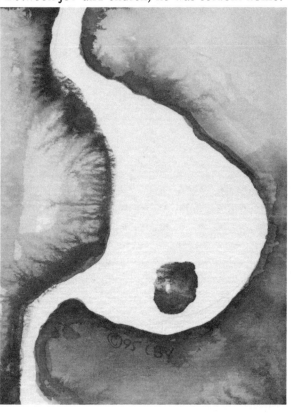

The woman asked about her last name; the teacher replied, adding, that her first name is Leonor. Indeed, the child from the classroom was this woman's oldest daughter! What a coincidence. The teacher informed her of the child's present living circumstances and invited her to come to school to see her.

Two aunts made the first visit to the school; they cried when they saw Leonor. She was nothing but a bag of bones, clothed in rags. Weekly visits ensued until the day arrived to carry out an escape. She could be removed from the home if beaten hard enough for a doctor to prove the abuse. The doctor certified eighty-two bruises all over her body. Leonor's father never believed the report.

Although she was no longer physically mistreated, Leonor's life with her birth mother proved to be difficult. Leonor felt bitter that her mother had not rescued her earlier. "I'd continually ask my mother why she'd allowed me to live with my father. Crying over her sewing machine— she sewed for a meager income—my mother would beg me to forgive her.

"I had become a hardened child; I didn't have friends. Angry at my father for never wanting to know what I experienced, my ability had changed. Intelligent in my early years, I returned to my mother retarded in development."

"But through all that time, I knew God as my friend," reflects Leonor in simple faith. "I didn't understand everything. My parents treated me badly, abused me in many ways. But in spite of mistreatment, God remained my friend.

"When living with my mother, I went to church with her. I didn't miss. When twelve, I began to teach children's classes. A missionary woman nudged me, noting my gift for working with children. On Monday evenings I would go to church for instruction, and on Saturday afternoons I shared my learnings with thirty neighborhood children. I sang in the church choir; I went out with the youth."

At age sixteen Leonor had an experience that changed her life. A small group from her Baptist church attended charismatic services in another church. Revival was touching all of Guatemala in 1963. Leonor, along with many others, was filled with the Holy Spirit. Though she interprets this renewal differently now as an adult reflecting back, she knows that it aided her struggle to let go of deep-harbored resentment for how childhood experiences had deformed her. It also called her to commitment and ministry.

Along with others, Leonor became active with this charismatic, nondenominational church. Rapid growth took place—from twelve struggling groups to over 200 churches. Committed youth prepared to become pastors and church workers through a newly-opened, three-year Bible Institute. Leonor entered the program in its first year. Another youth, Mario Mendez, also felt called to ministry. They learned to know each other in spite of the Institute's strict social codes. Allowed to talk together only five minutes after supper, they needed permission to be together otherwise. Graduation and marriage followed in 1968.

During the next ten years they raised a family and pastored churches both in Guatemala City and in smaller towns. These years were both good and difficult. Their four children—one son Rene, and three daughters, Bette, Karla and Kati—were born. Known and respected as a teacher and minister, Mario was involved in prophecy, healing, and liberation from demonic possession.

Leonor's call to ministry was also strong, though the ministry of women was barely recognized. In addition to caring for the growing family and supporting Mario, she also worked with women and did counselling and visitation. She taught children's classes and trained other teachers.

In the early '70s, charismatic revival moved into other denominations. After Mario traveled in Honduras, the Mendez family was invited to work in Mennonite churches there for two years. They did not interpret this as leaving their own church, but as extending the charismatic teaching and emphasis. In this transcultural, trans-church experience, they also acquired new emphases. In Honduras they saw the service orientation of their new group. They observed pastors who also had other employment. They found an "authentically human spirituality," Leonor said, which reconciled, rather than separated, reality with the spiritual.

Cracks began to appear in the Guatemala fortress of charismatic churches. Missionaries had little denominational identity. Being filled with the Holy Spirit had become central, rather than the life and ministry of Jesus. A new revival wave came from outside, often through foreign leaders. The church—noted for healings, miracles, and liberation—lacked a balanced or developed theology.

In addition, reports of sexual misconduct and scandal plagued key leaders during these years. While many tried to keep facts secret, the Mendez's were involved in disclosures. This prompted their exile from their own denomination. When they returned from Honduras no pastorate was available.

"These were times of pain and anguish, struggle and deception," Leonor recalls. "We felt called to pastor, but after empty promises, in reality there was no place for us. We felt uprooted and dislocated. Leaving the church in this way affected me deeply."

Leonor particularly remembers the birth of their last child, Kati, in 1978. She had just discovered that she had diabetes; delivery and recovery were very difficult. "We had just left the church. We were not economically stable. I felt like we had lost everything. I remember standing in the doorway of my little house, asking God, "*Why?*" Taught that illness and problems were signs of God's judgment, I had no idea why God should be punishing me."

"I felt like God was asking me to give up three things. First, my prestige; I thought I could live without that. I remember saying, 'I've given You my good name.' God also seemed to deprive us of economic security and privilege. Finally, the most painful—we were without a ministry. I remember crying out, 'But at least You stay with me, God. I cannot give You up.'

"This led me to evaluate who God was for me. I think this is what touches people when I speak now. I know God deeply, not because of my work or studies, but through all that I have experienced."

During this uncertain period, Mario and Leonor started a church which they could not sustain alone. Leaving this, they officially left the pastorate as a vocation. "Even so, my constant call is to be in the work of the church," Leonor said. They joined the Mennonites in Guatemala. Mario sold greeting cards, prior to beginning their own card production business.

This was the beginning of a new era for Leonor. The Mennonite church was casting about in the 1980s for its own identity in the midst of Central American oppression and social upheaval. What did its heritage of Anabaptism offer? What did being part of the kingdom of God mean among masses of Guatemalans who were deprived of life's basic necessities?

The Latin American Anabaptist Seminary (SEMILLA) was born in the mid-1980s. A seminary extension program open to leaders in all Central American countries, SEMILLA's central offices are in Guatemala City. Leonor was among the first to use this resource to continue theological study.

"I have always felt the urge to discover more. SEMILLA opened new doors. I have grown and matured. It's been a process, with cost. At first Mario resisted my study. He wouldn't fight it outright, but he'd plant obstacles. Not wanting to neglect my household, I prepared things at home before leaving to study. But I also couldn't give up studying in order to be fully absorbed in my children; I don't believe they resent my choices.

"We felt like we'd 'come home' in our chosen church," she says. "There are so many aspects that have felt right. My individualism has changed from a concept of '*God and me*' to one of '*community.*' We search for salvation together. I'm responsible for others in the community, and they're responsible for me. There is more freedom to be who God calls us to be. God is not static, but continues to speak to us, not through a church hierarchy, but in community consensus. We continue to learn on the way.

"The Gospel has to do with how we live. My faith must be relevant to my reality. To be the people of God, in daily life or corporate worship, and to discover the meaning of faithfulness—this is our great task. The task belongs to all of us together."

Seeking to be true to the Gospel, Central American Mennonite leaders began to realize they could not silence the gifts of church women. In 1985, a joint consultation and SEMILLA course on "Women in Ministry" was instrumental in leading to greater equality among women and men in the church. A written statement followed:

> We have helped to perpetuate attitudes that offend God and hurt women by imposing a feeling of unlimited and powerful authority only for the benefit of men and to the detriment of women...The pattern or model in which we find ourselves is not in agreement with the principles of community life, the community of faith and commitment, the people of God, nor the community of believers. As members of the body of Christ, we accept this historic challenge to work intensively in order that the barriers between men and women disappear and do not continue to be obstacles in the expression of God's kingdom.

[Study Course of SEMILLA, Costa Rica, June 1985]

The struggle for freedom for women in the churches continues alongside the struggle for freedom from oppressive forces in all areas of Central America. Leonor has known how to use her gifts to gain the respect and confidence of women and men, at this crucial time.

Leonor and Mario share pastoral responsibilities with a small team at the Shalom Mennonite church in Guatemala City. This is not a formal pastorate; they receive no remuneration. To leave the traditional structures has been difficult in some ways. "But," Leonor says, "we never had the idea of living off the church. Circumstances have helped to confirm this. Nevertheless, I can't imagine not working in the church."

Teaching and preaching ministries are most fulfilling for Leonor. She does both well. But churches needed time to accept her. "Now Shalom recognizes and utilizes my gifts. Not having sought this reinforces God's call. Some people have asked about ordination. I would value that if it reflects my church community's recognition of my pastoral gifts. But I am not interested, if it is only for a position."

She preaches frequently in Shalom and often in other local churches. She leads women's study groups and retreats. "I take on these assignments with a feeling of responsibility. I do not stand before any group without investing a lot of time in preparation and prayer. I feel fulfilled. When I see response in people—whether acceptance, repentance, or a call to greater commitment—I thank God."

Beyond local commitments, Leonor has spoken at women's retreats in Honduras and the United States. Her biggest surprise came when she was invited to preach at Mennonite World Conference in 1990. It was both a great honor and a sacrifice. Her fragile health, due to diabetes, complicated her travel.

"After I finished my sermon and sat quietly during the evening's final announcements, I realized again how faithful God has been. God has given back the three things I felt were taken away many years ago. The vocation of ministry had been returned. We now have a certain economic security; we need not wonder about food for breakfast. And my good name has returned. God owes me nothing!

"We've been through many crises. The past lingers like a corpse. To believe in people and in church structures has been hard. I've seen so much abuse of power—personal and spiritual. To reconcile what's happened in the past with the Gospel as we now know it has been difficult. But God has been faithful to permit me to see the present. Because of deep trust and community, I have not lost faith in God. I am grateful."

That sincerity depicts her gentle warmth. Leadership has fully replaced lethargy, making hers a story to tell.

Recent update: Leonor is now involved with the Casa Horeb worship group.

9

Christian Women of Belgium
Denise Peeters-LeBouleng and Daisy Van Cauwenberghe

Sylvia Shirk Charles[*]

> *Anticipate a focus on process. Conscious intents complement actions. As women reshape their place, the process transforms previous limits. Ecumenical cooperation often prompts a healthier view of differences among people.*

During my eight years in Belgium, some of my most rewarding and eye-opening experiences occurred through my involvement with an organization called Femmes Chretiennes de Belgique (Christian Women of Belgium). But, in 1981, as a newly-arrived Mennonite Board of Missions worker in Brussels, I lacked enthusiasm for such an option.

"The Christian Women of Belgium are holding a World Day of Prayer service this Thursday. Would you like to go?" That was our colleague Wilda Otto on the phone, telling me about the upcoming event. "Women from South America will be leading the prayers." She

---

[*]Sylvia Shirk Charles lived in Brussels, Belgium, from 1981 through 1988. Since then she completed a theology degree at Episcopal Divinity School in Cambridge, Massachusetts, and worked as an interpreter of Haitian Creole. She will leave the pastoral team at Waterford Mennonite Church in Goshen, Indiana, to become Campus Pastor at Goshen College in the summer of 1996.

explained to me where the service was to be held. Not knowing my new locale, I vaguely pictured women praying in a Brussels subway station. Unmotivated or preoccupied with a four-month-old baby and his older sister, I did not attend the World Day of Prayer that year.

I confess as well that my only previous association with the World Day of Prayer was knowing that Miriam, my mother-in-law, annually attended a service in Goshen, Indiana. Somehow, I had concluded that this was not an event for women of my generation, that nothing exciting for me was there. I was wrong.

Later, when I asked if Christian feminism existed in Belgium or who was involved, I was directed back to the Christian Women of Belgium. They were the planners, among other things, of the annual World Day of Prayer. I soon became involved in these events and learned about the varied facets of this dynamic group.

Women from various Christian groups formed the ecumenical Christian Women of Belgium in 1978. Organized on a national level, their concerns included to give voice, to nurture, to link, and to inspire Christian women. Knowing that common issues cannot be resolved only at denominational or national levels, the group recognized that issues of economy, politics, society, and ecology must also be addressed by continents and worldwide endeavor. Since all such issues concern women in a unique way, women must be fully involved in expressing their views and searching for solutions. "Our Christian faith and our ecumenical solidarity call us to this action," states an introductory brochure.

Formed as a national branch of the Ecumenical Forum of European Women, and related to the World Council of Churches (WCC), Christian Women of Belgium (CWB) works closely with international women's concerns addressed by the WCC's sub-unit on Women in Church and Society. The corresponding organization in North America is Church Women United; other continents or regions have national groups of this type too.

Why This Group?—Ecumenism among Protestants has grown since early in this century. The World Council of Churches officially formed in 1948. Vatican II, taking shape between 1962 and 1965, promised real changes for the Roman Catholic Church. However, for women in both Catholic and Protestant churches, little substantive change occurred. Belgian women's impatience with the slow pace of ecumenical progress motivated them to form CWB.

When I recently heard Denise Peeters-LeBoulenge, CWB cofounder, describe the beginnings of CWB in this way, I wanted to smile. As I know her, Denise likes to see things move and change. She stirs up what is needed for women and the church. When we worked together in CWB, I had often been inspired by Denise's clarity of vision and her commitment to peace and justice.

But we were different. She was Roman Catholic, Belgian, middle class, and older than my parents, while I was a Mennonite North American, working class, young mother. Yet the convictions we shared allowed us to communicate readily from day one. Denise's gift of listening and her ability to understand those different from herself made her a natural for ecumenical work.

Denise says she was a feminist from the start. As tradition dictated, her brothers were given university education; she was not. She married and raised a family. When the children were older, Denise and her husband agreed to switch roles. She was employed for the first time, becoming involved in planning conventions.

Later, Denise became a commission member of the World Union of Catholic Women's Organizations, based in Brussels. Her commission's duty focused on ecumenism. Well into adulthood, she learned for the first time about Christians other than Roman Catholics. She was sent to Lutheran and Methodist women's conventions and later invited to a 1977 consultation of Church Women Executives held in Glion, Switzerland.

At the Glion meeting, Denise said, European women realized that they were not collaborating on regional issues in ways African, Asian, and American women did. They sent an open letter to Christian women in Europe asking for response from those who wished to form a European group. A first meeting, for which Denise was a primary organizer, was held in Brussels in 1978.

There, Daisy Van Cauwenberghe, a Protestant woman, entered the story of CWB. She and Denise quickly sensed their common interest in forming a Belgian group to bring together Catholic and Protestant women. With Daisy and Denise as co-founders, the Ecumenical Forum of European Christian Women was born, as well as a Flemish-language sister group to CWB.

"My marriage," Daisy said, "is the basis of my interest in ecumenical work. I hoped that what my husband Denys and I experience in our Protestant-Catholic marriage might also be the experience of other Christians working together."

Having met Daisy's husband, and having seen how they live side-by-side with complete respect for one another's commitments, helped me to appreciate Daisy's ecumenical interest. I knew also that Daisy had paid a price for countering tradition when she, from a middle class Swiss Protestant family, entered a mixed marriage in the early 1950s. Not welcome to worship together in either the Catholic or Protestant church, she and Denys had found a spiritual home among similar couples who met monthly.

Daisy also enjoyed other groups. "I had become fed up with being a housewife, and with women's minimal involvement in the Belgian church," she explained. She met with a group called Presence, whose members were mostly Protestant women. And during the 1970s, Daisy began to attend a Protestant church in spite of its somewhat authoritarian Mennonite pastor.

Daisy caused change by actively opening and entering doors of opportunity. She says she isn't a fighter like Denise. But I have experienced her profound energy and depth of commitment toward progress in ecumenical and international efforts. Her practical, matter-of-fact style contributes to smooth operation within CWB.

Ecumenism in Belgium—"Now in your religion, Madame," the visiting social worker asked, choosing her words with care, "is it the Virgin Mary that you don't believe in, or the Pope, or both?" She had come from the National Office for Children for the routine visit to a family with a newborn. After a good look at our little Daniel, she had asked about his eating habits, and advised me that having him sleep so close to the window above street noise was bad for his nerves. Now she probed her curiosity about Mennonites. During eight years in Belgium, I met many others who had never spoken to a non-Catholic Christian.

The Belgian's experience, while different in detail, alerted me to my insular experience growing up in Lancaster County, Pennsylvania. There, virtually everyone knew of Mennonites, whether or not they liked or understood them. We had our Mennonite summer camp, bought groceries from a Mennonite, shopped at Harry Good's store—where Mennonite ministers received a discount—even though Harry was a different kind of Mennonite from us. Our car was insured by a

Mennonite insurance company, bought from a Mennonite Chevy dealer, and sold later to a Mennonite used car dealer. But our dentist was a "worldly" person. Whew! I was sort of glad for a breather, for broader exposure.

In Belgium, the religious demographics are quite different. In 1980 Christians were 90.9% of the population. Of those, less than one percent belong to Protestant or related groups. There are more Muslims and more atheists than Protestants in Belgium, according to the *World Christian Encyclopedia.*

Dealing daily with people of other denominations marks experience for Protestants in Belgium. But Denise Peeters was middle-aged before she met non-Roman Catholics, the first time outside Belgium. Intent to form an ecumenical group within Belgium, CWB had to face the major disproportion of Catholics to Protestants.

Attitudes among Christian women needed challenge too. Denise found many in Catholic churches apathetic. Daisy knew of Protestant women's reticence to work hand-in-hand with Catholics—their historical oppressors—who continued to dominate the religious and political scene. Indeed, some women supported the male-oriented structures in both Catholic and Protestant Churches which failed to recognize and support CWB.

Amidst religious divisions, CWB set a standard for mutual respect and cooperation. Leadership would draw from both groups, nearly equally. To provide a balance in meeting places, speakers, and resources entailed care. With relatively few of us Protestants, I was regularly invited to plan and lead activities. For my first assignment, I shared some of my husband Robert's slides about Haiti, for a 1983 World Day of Prayer celebration.

I began attending CWB activities more regularly. Together, Daisy, Denise, and I planned a study day on women and men in the church, sponsored by my workplace—the Brussels Mennonite Center. Both were valuable resource people because of the work each had already done on the theme through CWB. I was active with the CWB leadership group from 1985-88.

Feminism in the Churches—"The brothers on the Belgian Mennonite Council have said that they prefer not to have women attend their meetings," colleague Jean Gerber and I were told in 1981. We had just met with this long-standing body. I was angry and frustrated. We had come from North America with a mandate to collaborate with the Mennonite Council. I did not expect them to object to meeting with us. But Belgium proved to be no different from the Mennonite church in which I had grown up. It too drew lines—to exclude women from decision-making but to include their ministry of service.

Daisy discovered a similar short supply of women when she attended national meetings of the United Protestant Church in the 1970s. The Belgian Protestant church's 1977 study on the place of women said that a woman should not stand in the pulpit. What a contrast to Protestantism in Geneva, where Daisy had women friends in the pastorate. But patterns are changing—a young woman recently became the pastor of the church Daisy attends.

Denise and Daisy's perceptions varied. Denise, who grew up with an all-male Catholic clergy, knew from ecumenical circles about change among some Protestants regarding women's ordination. Daisy thought that, in light of emerging opportunities, Protestant women had no excuse for inactivity in today's church. She expected Protestant women to encourage Catholic women who experience so many obstacles to ministry. But Denise observed, "I'm convinced that we are all up against the same problem—patriarchy." She wrote recently about this "hierarchal mold that has done us all so much wrong."

CWB provides space outside male-dominated hierarchies, synods, and councils for women to minister and grow. It is also a place for women to gain confidence and skill to later apply within traditional church structures.

Such growth occurred for me, too. In 1987, the CWB women recommended that I preach at the centennial celebration of the World Day of Prayer. A combined service for all of Belgium was to be held in Saint Michael's cathedral in Brussels. All the church hierarchies, as well as the Queen, were to be invited. "Me?" I asked. "Sure," they said. "You have some seminary training." So by God's grace I did it. Since then, I have completed seminary and am employed in pastoral work. Whenever sermon delivery makes me nervous, I need only recall that day in the crowded cathedral to regain confidence.

Daisy, in 1988, was invited to co-lead the commission for adult education for the United Protestant Church of Belgium. They have formed a dynamic working group, whose collegial working style, Daisy says, is patterned after CWB. Their four training sessions over the past two years have attracted record-breaking participation. The group is being recognized as one of the few lively entities within the church. Recently, they led a day-long session of the national church's annual synod. Both Daisy and Denise point to these developments as an outgrowth of the work of CWB.

"Why did you want to work on women's issues within the church?" I asked Daisy and Denise. Both replied that they saw a need to work at issues on all fronts. In many ways the church seemed to lag behind society. Denise is active in various national women's organizations. She has sat on the Council for Emancipation under the Secretary of State for the Belgian government. Daisy, with a sigh, says, "Maybe I should have gone into politics. Maybe that's where some real changes can happen." Her daughter not long ago came within one vote of winning a local election in Geneva.

Hearing them, I pondered the difference between their point of view and my own background. I was taught to avoid politics. The Kingdom of God, not society at large, was where we raise our voices or work to change structures. I do not know Mennonite women in North America who are active within political structures, as is Denise. I do know some, however, who are political outside the structures. They protest arms production and advocate for more justice in United States government policies in the two-thirds world, to mention only two areas.

CWB Activities—"I'm going to the Ecumenical Day tomorrow with Jean and Daisy," I told Robert one Friday in 1982, as we coordinated schedules. "Little Sophie will come with us, and Laura and Daniel will stay with you." A host of priests, plus a lone religious sister, organize Ecumenical Day, sponsored by the National Catholic Commission for Ecumenism.

CWB was invited to join the discussion of "Women and Men in the Church." Denise was on a panel during the closing session. She asked the group to respond by rising to their feet whenever they affirmed comments in a series. "If you believe that all the twenty-six Gospel references to Jesus and women are affirmative of women, stand up!" she said. Most of us were on our feet immediately. But as the affirmations became more political—"For women to be faithful to their God-given gifts, some will be prophets and preachers"—some of the brothers became less quick to rise. "That Denise Peeters is a dangerous woman," warned a Belgian priest friend. But CWB continued its dialogue with the Commission and regularly attended subsequent ecumenical days.

"Marty," I asked my neighbor one day, "would you be willing to help with children for part of a worship I'm planning with Christian Women of Belgium?" I needed her because she had musical skills and she could bring her many children. CWB was planning the annual World Day of Prayer and hoped to add some vigor to the liturgy. The Gospel text from Matthew 21:12-17 included a group of children who disturb the chief priests and scribes by singing. Our idea was to have singing, dancing children interrupt the usually solemn World Day of Prayer celebration. I think we pulled it off.

Marty had held a little rehearsal with the children so that all could more or less sing the chorus "Sing Hosanna!" while holding hands and shuffling along. Our little troupe burst in on the worshipers during the Gospel reading. They danced to a circle in the front of the room. While dancing, charming three-year-old Libby moved into a liturgical floral arrangement, carefully laid out in a huge bowl of water. This created a big puddle where the children needed to sit for the remainder of the service. For me, this was one of the most memorable, joyful annual celebrations.

CWB planned other projects and activities. We supplied information about women and children in South Africa, where Daisy's sister worked as a missionary. Many attended a day of Bible-study on the theme, "Women Bearers of Hope." For several years a group of women and men, lay and clergy, Protestant and Catholic met to study theology. Another group intent on "Getting to Know Feminist Theology" studied the French translation of Fiorenza's *In Memory of Her*. CWB women volunteered at Dar Al Amal, a cultural center and employment cooperative for immigrant women in Brussels. In 1986 members gathered to found the European Society of Women for Theological Research in Magliaso, Switzerland. CWB maintained close ties with the Ecumenical Forum for European Christian Women. Now including twenty-five countries, this group held assemblies in Switzerland in 1982, Finland in 1986, and England in 1990.

"We need to encourage women in local churches to become more active," someone expressed. Denise shared a study guide developed in Canada by a Catholic group. We adapted the study to a Belgian, ecumenical setting. Working as a team, several of us re-wrote each session. We advertized the 1987 workshop—"Women and the Churches"—in our newsletter. Each of the six sessions, held at the Brussels Mennonite Center, was led by two from our team, a Catholic and a Protestant. Each meeting included analysis, experience, and a closing meditation. And when the course ended, we published the study guide. "Will anyone really make use of this booklet?" I silently mused as Daisy and Denise decided to print 150 copies. A second printing followed!

Looking Ahead—"What future do you see for CWB, and what dreams do you have for the group?" I recently asked Daisy and Denise. Denise dreams of being heard by the broader church and of sharing more widely the vision of CWB. "I'd like them to understand that we are not seeking power for power's sake," she says, "but that we want to have power in order to share it. We'd like to achieve true partnership."

"Looking to the future," Daisy says, "I see a need for a group like CWB only for women. As CWB grows, women will bring about true ecumenism."

As I finished visiting with these two remarkable women, I knew how blessed I had been to work closely with Christian Women of Belgium. I had witnessed, firsthand, the struggle and the endurance of women whose Christian faith is very important. My own development as a Christian minister with ecumenical vision had known support and encouragement from a group of sisters.

When I settled in the Boston area in 1988, one of my first stops was the office of Church Women United. No one was there, and no one replied to the note I left. Determined, I have found women in mixed-faith groups with whom to share important values. And now I believe that when I'm in Goshen and Miriam goes to the World Day of Prayer service, I'll join her.

10

Worship That Asks Probing Questions

Liz

Nelda Thelin[*]

Anticipate oft'-hidden reality that can challenge assumptions. While what women think may not always be reflected in what they do, to value their perceptions of their responses matters. Do you more often choose to be acted upon or to take action?

Sunday—a time for church, for visiting friends, for relaxation, for families to gather. I like Sundays. But to be quite honest, I sometimes struggle inwardly over going outwardly to church. To say this aloud risks judgment, of course. "What would people think" about a person working with a church organization who would prefer to stay home to read or reflect about God, while her husband and children go off to worship God at church?

Sunday services are usually the same here in Transkei; they bore or frustrate me. The brothers read the scripture; they preach and pray.

---

[*]Nelda Thelin has worked in several African countries, for some years with Mennonite Central Committee and more recently with the United Church of Christ. She is excited about the Umtata Women's Theology Group that studies texts, translates booklets into the Xhosa language, and sponsor's women's conferences.

The sisters sit and listen with respect. And what of content read, preached, prayed, or sung? It refers primarily to him, his, and brothers. I feel very much like a spectator at a worship service for the brothers.

When I feel magnanimous, I find communion services enjoyable. Brothers, who usually sit to be served, become the servers. They serve with such pride. After all, they are the elected leaders of the congregation. And the sisters? They sit and are served. What a revolution!

At other times I feel hurt or angry. I might hold firmly to the bench, to thwart the temptation to get up and walk out. These are times when the Spirit of God becomes distinctly real to me, because matters of justice surface. Something happens. Perhaps the trigger is a single reference to *brothers*. Or perhaps there's a reference to *blessed peacemakers* being called "the sons of God." When that occurs—as it did last Sunday—I "switch off." My mind wanders as I look about at other people seated in the pews.

In the front sit the young people. Almost all of them are teenage girls. I wonder if they notice how this service refers to brothers only. Probably not. I wonder if any of them feels called to preach, feels an urge to some full-time ministry in the church. Probably not. But I should ask. Who else would plant such seed?

Behind the girls are the sisters. One of them fills in willingly for an organist who does not arrive or know the right tune. Another responds if no young people appear to gather the offering. I wonder if one of them ever wishes to be a minister or feels called to preach. Probably not. I should ask. But who might answer with integrity?

To my left is Allen. Allen and his wife, Liz, are from Scotland. Liz does not often come to church. She calls herself a "fallen away Presbyterian." As a chain smoker, she coughs a lot and has been hospitalized for a lung condition.

But Liz is a very special person. Every day Liz can be found at the refuse dump. No, she isn't looking for clothes or food cast off by the rich. She goes to be a Presence, to relate with the many women, men, and children who live there. They, by nature reciprocate.

When Liz and Allen first arrived, Liz offered to teach the women at the dump to sew. At first they met in a friend's garage. But that caused the women to miss out on the loads refuse which arrived every morning on dump trucks. So, Liz and the women built their own special sewing shack at the dump.

After working at the dump every day, Liz became oblivious to the environment which first-time visitors find so shocking and repulsive. The stench from the nightsoil dump bothered her only on extremely hot, humid days—days void of a diffusing breeze. The crowded, compact, squalid, tin and cardboard shelters worried her most when cold weather arrived, causing people to build fires in order to stay warm. Children's welcoming smiles always contradicted their smudgy cheeks, sordid bodies, and drab, tattered clothing.

People "on the outside" commonly viewed people from the dump as lazy or drunkards. The people at the dump easily persuaded Liz that such was *not true*! To her, they were homeless individuals. Through some misfortune, not usually of their own making, they had lost their jobs or been unable to find work.

In contrast to those who self-righteously judged, Liz became deeply involved in the lives of the people. She knew when a baby was born, when a woman was beaten by her husband, or when a young lad found something special in a new bag of trash. Liz also discovered that when someone died, no one helped with arrangements for a coffin or burial. She learned that when a person from the dump became sick, hospital or clinic staff had little time for them. They could be kept waiting for hours.

Eventually, Liz decided to start a small clinic where she could dispense some basic medicines. She offered first aid to small children. Their feet were inevitably cut as they walked barefoot on broken glass—the very foundation of the dump site.

One morning I visited Liz at the dump. She was busy cleaning sores and changing dressings on cuts from the day before. A trusting three-year-old girl held up her foot. Liz, kneeling on the dirt floor, gently removed the old, filthy bandage. She cleaned the wound and placed a fresh, clean dressing on the wee foot. As she worked, Liz carried on a one-way conversation, in her Scottish brogue. While the child comprehended little of the vocabulary, she clearly understood Liz's cheerful tone of voice and loving concern. This, I thought, was a true act of worship, an active ministry.

Meanwhile, back at the Sunday worship service, the minister was winding down. The Sri Lankan woman doctor seated on my other side dabbed at her eyes. She obviously had been touched by something the minister said.

Perhaps I had missed an important insight—but I had also communed with God through my reflection on Liz. Or, who knows, perhaps she had envisioned another "Liz," off in Colombo.

Just perhaps, whatever the insight, those at worship received equally valid messages or Wisdom from the Spirit of God. Prompted while present at church—does the location matter? Perhaps not. Perhaps I should ask Liz.

11

Hopes and Struggles of the Church in South Asia

*Prakai Nontawasee**

> *Anticipate hearing an Asian talk about her own people's journey, insights, and efforts. Listen to where they are, knowing that failure to hear often indicates lack of knowledge, patience, or willingness to extend another her authority.*

[The following is excerpted, with permission, from the author's presentation to the November 1989 meeting in Chicago, of CIM (Council of International Ministries), with which Mennonite Missions agencies are active.]

South Asia covers a vast territory—just look at a globe. To attempt to speak about several main issues from such a broad continent is risky. But look again at the globe and compare the space I refer to with the United States. As writers might speak of "Mennonites in the United States," so I introduce churches in part of South Asia. Both groups measure but a

---

*Prakai Nontawasee has been the Vice Moderator of the Church of Thailand. Other leadership opportunities have included: chairperson of the ECPAI (End Child Prostitution in Asia), Presidium of CCA (Christian Conference of Asia), Central committee member of WCC (World Council of Churches).

small minority of the total population.

This window into churches in South Asia—India, Pakistan, Nepal, Bangladesh, Sri Lanka, Burma, and Thailand—only begins the task. Think of it as a mini-collage, a glance at the spectrum, a filter that lets many items pass while a few are briefly caught to examine but an angle. Think also of "church" more broadly than people gathered for worship. "Church is where the heart is" might better translate the context of human interaction amidst hopes and struggles. As the prophet Jeremiah knew, "to know God is to do justice."

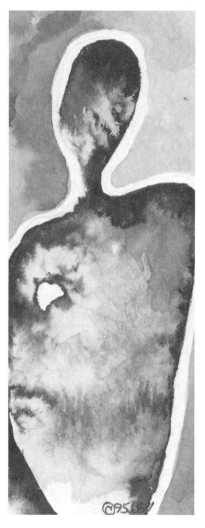

A current, dominant feature of the Asian scene centers in human rights violations. The majority of people who suffer in this way are women and children. Marginalized people continue to be sinned against by all who relegate any person to the periphery, by all who deprive another from realizing her dreams, and by all who keep another ignorant of her basic right to wholeness.

For example, in India, Pakistan, and Bangladesh the problem of dowry continues to negatively impact many women and the family unit. A dowry is the "gift" demanded of a bride when she marries. Failure to appease her husband's family can lead to her harassment, torture, murder or suicide. Church and women's groups actively counter this societal pattern.

Another misuse of human rights involves tourism in Sri Lanka, the Philippines, and Thailand. While male tourists ostensibly come to enjoy Sun, Sea and Sand, they often expect sex as part of the package. A root cause of prostitution is poverty, with its related problems— hunger, drugs, crime, and oppression. That all major religions, as practiced, sanction male control of women, is further cause.

In addition to exploiting people, tourism pollutes nature or the broader environment plus it destroys culture. Several months ago Christian Churches of Asia (CCA), Federation of Asian Bishops Conference (FABC) and the Ecumenical Coalition on Third World Tourism sponsored an Asian conference. Participants committed themselves to expose and root out the evils of tourism.

Problems of poverty affect Pakistan, Bangladesh and Nepal, also. The interplay of poverty and rights cries from the printed page. From *Human Rights in Nepal* (1989), we learn the following: "The Nepalese law has not given education or property rights to the daughter, as it has to sons . . . the daughter is to survive at the mercy of father or brothers." For the two other countries, poverty is acute because of how economic structures are begun or dominated by capitalist powers.

As is true elsewhere, some Asians have also become self-centered when competition increases. Consumerism and materialism add to the plight. Caught up in the mentality that "more is better," each seeks more. Power linked to possession or selfish control over products or people then leads to division. The gap widens between the majority poor, who lack power that matters, and the minority rich, who may deny how their wealth deprives others.

Political upheaval adds to the struggle for Asian people. Burma's situation illustrates the problem. Along the borders between Thailand and Burma, camps of Burmese students, who fled their country during bloody demonstrations in Rangoon in 1988, remain. Following arrests of pro-democracy party leaders and members, fear prevails among the people. Oppression continues. High costs of basic food like rice, coupled with uncontrolled inflation, aggravate the situation. A ray of hope glimmers as students attempt to open jungle universities.

While Laos is opening its door for more connection with neighboring countries, Kampuchea appears less certain whether to remain isolated or not. The latter's relation with Vietnam grows ever more complex. Whether Thailand will be able to bring the involved parties together remains to be seen. Further, church-government relations in Vietnam also remain guarded. The region is "tenuous." For Christians either to ignore dilemmas or pessimistically excuse themselves from grappling with issues is less than responsible. Even those halfway around the world hardly dare look the other way.

A window into Asian struggles and hopes must include sensitivity toward refugees. This involves understanding both obvious and subtle reasons for, as well as the hazards of, mass migration. While Thailand, Malaysia and Hong Kong continue to cope with "boat people," the number of Laotian and Cambodian refugees is decreasing. Vietnam will be asked to reduce the rate of refugee departures. A new ray of hope calls Asian churches to involvement in repatriation programs, whether through Christian Churches of Asia or the World Council of Churches. For example, the Khao I Dang camp, on the Thai border, will be turned into a Voluntary Repatriation Training Center with a three-year, Khmer language training program.

But repatriation, if forced, prompts further debate and pain. Some host countries meet the resulting problems more sensitively than others. Openness and exchange might help. A screening process is needed to determine each refugee's plight. Some genuinely flee from destructive circumstances while a few opportunists might migrate for revenge or to further oppress some target group.

So what shapes hope for South Asian churches? Christians are surrounded by dominant religions—Buddhism in Thailand and Sri Lanka, Hinduism in India, Islam in Pakistan and Bangladesh. To engage with people of other faiths might cause intimidation for a minority. Sharing in local, national, and regional efforts for the common good brings hope. As Christians join across religious faiths to confront oppression and exploitation, they activate God's liberating and redemptive power.

One example of joint, regional activity centers on reconciling the ethnic conflict between Sinhalese and Tamils in Sri Lanka. The indigenous Sinhalese group resents the Tamils who over several centuries have either invaded from southern India or been brought there, as by British rulers. Matters of history and economics (such as Tamil "second-class" status) aggravate the problem more than the fact that most Sinhalese are Buddhists and Tamils are Hindu.

Out of basic humanitarian concern or because of religious principles for justice, Christians and people of other living faiths will respond. With their worldview broader than their own borders, neighboring countries become engaged with peace-making dimensions. Thai and Sinhalese Buddhist priests and lay people initiated such a program. ACFOD (Asian Cultural Forum on Development) then collaborated with six national/international organizations for a symposium between different Buddhist groups. A follow-up program included non-Buddhists. A nonviolent training program was also planned.

Communication is a second factor of hope. As church groups and other non-governmental organizations establish honest and open dialogue with each other and with governmental organizations working on similar issues, understanding deepens. Information is shared and life stories are told and heard. Along with trust and closeness, credible dialogue follows.

A third sign of hope amidst struggle is willingness to be in solidarity with the poor and oppressed. For Christians, to be in solidarity means to drink the cup of suffering through prayerful action. This leads to true friendship. It empowers us to see the light, as we wait for the dawn. To be in solidarity means to form a network of mutual sharing of information, commitment, and support.

God is indeed in solidarity with us. Full of hope, because of the incarnated Christ—"Immanuel, God with us"—we join efforts with various others to address struggles.

[The following is Prakai's poetic testimony concerning hope and suffering.]

"The Graveyard Near the River Kwai"*
At the graveyard near the River Kwai I stood,
Reflecting on the suffering death of many men—
    the prisoners of war.
Falling into the pit of bitterness, hatred, and despair,
My heart and soul weighed down
    with a heavy stone of compassionate grief.
In the camp, a man, frail and torn, found the hidden Bible.
He shared God's word and prayerful fellowship
    with the helpless, sick, and dying.
A Miracle happened—

---

*The area near the River Kwai in Kanchanaburi province in Thailand is the place where Japanese soldiers kept World War II prisoners of war and forced them to construct the railway from the Thailand border to connect with a Burmese railway.

More love and care blossomed;
More endurance for the tortured prevailed;
More kind words melted with warmth of heart for the enemies.
> One night POWs even entertained them
> with a tin-can concert.

The first and the last communion was held.
Using rice and water—the only food for survival,
Under the mango tree where I stood,
> The war was ended.
> The men were gone.
> But, the cross in the graveyard
>> Still bears the victory over
>> All wars and struggling.

12

Bethania: Child Woman of the Streets

Aruna Gnanadason[*]

Anticipate an understanding of culture beyond formal learning. To see a child within the social forces affecting her calls for keen observation.

She walks with a confident dignity;
She talks with an air of grace;
She is but a child-woman,
Bethania is her name.

When a mere eight years old, she ran away from home.
That "prison-like" existence she could endure no more—
Raped five times and repeatedly harassed by a cruel father,
Plus from a helpless, worn out mother,
       only more battery, more pain.

Friends and companions she found on the streets of Recife,
As she joined the eleven million street children of Brazil.
Living together on the edge of uncertainty and hunger

---

[*]Aruna Gnanadason, from India, currently heads the World Council of Churches (Geneva, Switzerland) Programme Unit III: Justice, Peace, and Creation, which includes programs with women.

She found new, acceptance, a new community,
    and, most of all, love.

Arrested for stealing a piece of bread to ease her hunger,
In a remand home, she learned about life.
Escaping that "prison,"
    she entered the world a hardened criminal.
This she had learned: to ruthlessly survive.

Pregnant at the tender age of fifteen,
In a context of lustful greed, and with a handful of coins;
Caught in a quagmire of insecurity, fear and constant hunger
She knew she could live no more in yet another "prison."

Hesitant, in a halfway home, she sought someone who truly cared.
    For her the right to selfhood, for her unborn the right to life.
Now with her child she's found companionship,
    a sense of meaning,
That prompts her to find life for others
    when left to fend alone.

She walks with a confident dignity;
She talks with an air of grace;
She is but a child-woman,
Bethania is her name.

Geneva, Switzerland
April 17, 1992

[Inspired by Bethania, a rehabilitated street child Aruna learned to know during the Anglican Women's Encounter on the Ecumenical Decade held in Salvador de Bahia, Brazil, 29 March to 3 April 1992.]

13

The Street People
Eggrinah Kaliyati and
Inez Caldewood's Stories

as told to Doris Dube[*]

Anticipate thinking about the narratives by which key people in this story live. People in many cities and countries find coping with life to be difficult. Social fabric and historical setting affect them too.

The scum of the earth! I saw his kind everyday in Bulawayo, Zimbabwe. They roamed the streets, set up home on the pavement, begged shamelessly—and were probably an embarrassment to the government when visitors toured the city. The public gave them names without end. Dirty, smelly, and anything but attractive . . . yet one person in particular arrested my attention.

The time was just after 7:30 p.m. I'd been to the railway station to say goodbye to a Zambian friend. The train had been rather late and I really was anxious to get home. So was my son Davie who had plans for the evening.

All was well with us. I was basking in a new relationship with my

---

*Doris Dube is a teacher, homemaker, and writer. A Zimbabwean national, she lives in Bulawayo with her family. She is an active member of the Brethren in Christ church. This chapter was submitted by Doris's friend Nelda Thelin, whose story appears earlier.

Creator. My life had been undergoing change. Prayer renewed my outlook. The broader world and the people around me were much the same, yet I saw them with different eyes. Joyful, my mind seemed tuned to God.

When stopped at a red light, I saw him. He wasn't that different from other street people I'd seen before. However, as he ambled past, under the load of all that he owned, something happened that I couldn't explain. I'd barely pulled ahead, as the light turned green, when I heard a Voice. It was clear, distinct, and resonating with command, "Go back! Go!"

Stubbornly I drove on, more than two blocks. The Voice persisted, "Go back! Go back."

I turned to my son and said, "Davie, we have to go back . . ."

"Why, Mum? It's getting late and . . ."

"I know, Davie, but we must return. That man, you know. We have to go back to him."

"But, Mum, why? What's so special about him? He's just one of the street squatters. What do you want to do?"

"Davie, I don't know. I just feel compelled. God is speaking to me. I need to check this out."

"Mum, how can you be so sure?"

I turned and headed back until I stopped near the railway station. The area was crowded with street walkers. Now, as I looked at them huddled under their dirty rags, I couldn't tell which one I had seen at the red light.

Dipping my hand into my pocket, I found a dollar coin. I went into a nearby cafe and bought two buns. Armed with these, I approached one of the mounds of misery. I lifted the rags and a face popped out. Silently, I handed him the two buns and a fifty-cent coin. He shook his head and said, "I have no money."

"I'm not selling. It's my gift to you. Take it."

With dirty, gnarled hands, he reached out and grabbed the buns and coin. In horror I watched as he fumbled among the rags, brought out a dirty old tin, opened it—revealing some repulsive, moldy stuff—then threw in the buns, closed the tin, and settled down for a night's rest of wakefulness.

"Why are you throwing the buns away? Don't you want them? Why are you putting them in with that dirt?"

"I do want them. I am saving them for tomorrow. This tin is where I keep my food."

The moment was pregnant with emotion. I looked at the poor man and saw a child of God, a child of the universe. I looked at the others nearby and saw my brothers, my sisters, my children. Underneath all those rags and misery were people of beauty. At the same time, they were in tatters. Their bellies were empty. They had no comfortable beds or warm blankets to protect them from the elements.

They had nothing! Absolutely nothing! How that realization hurt. How my heart cried out to those dear human beings.

Then, Davie, who earlier remained in the car, joined me. With tears streaming down my cheeks, I returned silently to the car. We went home in silence, too. Having seen a sight that defies description, we each had an inner battle to fight and win.

That night there was little sleep at our house. Each of my four children went to their closets to gather items of clothing. I did the same with my husband's and my clothes. Adding some blankets, we had quite a bundle. Prayers that night cared for the hungry and homeless.

The next day birthed a "kitchen on wheels." Working as a family team, my children and I cooked food and headed for the region near the railway station. One child led the team with a bucket of soapy water for washing hands. The rest of us followed, dishing out food into plastic ice-cream containers. After feeding the people, we gave them clothes and blankets. We returned home with hearts heavier than when we had begun.

The next day at the same time—7:30 p.m.—we went out again. The time was right for finding a large number of people, having returned from begging routes into the city centre and outskirts. They were settling down for the night.

Taken aback, we were greeted happily by them in their rags! None of the clothes distributed the day before were to be seen. They'd been sold for food and other essentials. Later, one of my sons suggested a solution to partly meet our goal. Whenever a garment was given, the person's rags were exchanged. We continued the feeding scheme for about four months. I was soon known as the "Food Woman."

One Friday evening, we were out as usual. Mr. Mukesh, a Christian from our congregation who had just said goodbye to a friend at the railway station, spotted our car. He thought perhaps we had had a breakdown so looked for me to offer his help. What a sight met him!

And what an explanation followed.

By the next Sunday, Mukesh had shared the story with our pastor and other members of our church. During the service, other people were moved to give in cash or kind. Within a short time, we had cartons and cartons of food and clothing, plus piles of blankets.

At this time another dimension of Divine concern for people was revealed. Rev. Avery of the Zimbabwe Christian Mission had just returned from a visit to South Africa. There he had observed a feeding scheme called a "Soup Kitchen." We decided to adopt that style. Methodists offered their property. On June 1, 1987, the first Soup Kitchen in Bulawayo opened at the Methodist Centre on Main Street.

By then media people were informed and ready to air the story. As the vision was shared with churches in Bulawayo, seven denominations responded: Roman Catholic, Presbyterian, Dutch Reformed, Bulawayo Christian Centre, Anglican, Disciples of Christ, and Methodist with each denomination serving one day a week. A cooperative pattern emerged for church members and other volunteers. One full-time and three part-time cooks were employed.

People were fed one daily, midday meal, using a ticket system. Individuals and groups bought tickets, distributed them to street beggars, and directed them to the Methodist Centre. The ticket was given in exchange for a meal. This system was later phased out when we realized that needy people could be missed by those who issued tickets. Later, the needy received a card at the door which they surrendered when leaving. This provided a record of the number served. Everyday, 60-180 people ate at the Soup Kitchen.

[Dube reasons that if one person like Eggrinah Kaliyati hears and responds to the "Voice" of the poor, other people will be more likely to respond to that "Voice" also.]

"A Further Dimension of the Story" as told by Rev. Richard Wilde— Truly, the above is not the end of the story. It is but a small window into a larger picture yet to unfold.

Even before Eggrinah Kaliyati started her "Kitchen on Wheels," the plight of the less privileged of society was a prime concern to many in Bulawayo. Rodney Capon, a member of the Main Street Methodist Church, had prodded Christians to address this concern. Under his leadership, all the Bulawayo churches were invited to pool resources, to minister together with the needy. People knew that in the city centre some street walkers begged from church to church on a fairly regular basis. To discourage this, an alternative had to be found. One option was a soup kitchen.

In another corner of the city of Bulawayo, Inez Caldewood, a member of the St. John's Anglican church thought of another option—to establish a shelter to house all destitute people. Although it was a big project, she believed it could be done. Her eyes had been opened; others shared the vision.

From about mid-1989 to early 1990, pieces of a jigsaw started to fall into place. Mayor of Bulawayo, Councillor Ndlove, called a meeting. Church groups, members of the Bulawayo Residents' Association, the Social Welfare Organization, political representatives, City Council and other citizens were invited. The mayor's message to the Bulawayo residents was quite simple—a clear call to clean the city and remove the beggars from the street. How and when was yet to be determined.

Time was ripe for action. The Isolation Unit, formerly a smallpox complex, had stood idle for over twenty years. No more cases of the disease had been reported in the country. Good buildings stood on four hectares of land. By winter of 1990, plans were underway to clean, rewire, and generally prepare these for use. In November the first group of residents moved into what is now called the Bulawayo Shelter in Thorngrove. Many have come and gone since.

Residents are a broad mix of characters. Selection gives preference to people over forty. Most are very secretive about their past. Most had lost their jobs. After spending years on the street, they were ashamed to go home in tatters. Others had destroyed their marriages; they were left without a sense of belonging.

A screening procedure precedes admittance for residents. Rules of conduct stipulate no alcohol, smoking, or sexual intimacy among them. Caring is not limited to physical needs; spiritual life matters for residents and volunteers. Bible Studies occur on Wednesday evenings. Now a few former beggars have become church leaders. All residents must be willing to assist with simple manual labor in the buildings or with grounds. Above all, they know that the Shelter is not a permanent home. They are to move on at the end of three months—hopefully equipped with a needed survival skill.

Today the Bulawayo Shelter thrives as a community. A visitor to the complex finds groups of people engrossed in varied projects. They produce beautiful works of art to sell in the city centre. Others are occupied with carpet-making, carpentry, gardening, and shoe construction or repair. Opportunity to be productive has had a very positive effect on most of the residents. With a little money in hand, they have exchanged the drab rags of a beggar for clean attire and new dignity. With self-respect restored, many leave the Shelter to start a new life.

Options are open to them. All people have an extended family somewhere. Plagued by utter poverty, many people are reluctant to go home to friends and family. However, once redeemed from the status of street-beggar, many are willing to return home to pursue life. Social Services assist by providing a free pass on public transport.

Some opt for Government resettlement schemes. In those they become new people in new areas. Others join the Lutheran World Federation Cooperative based in Nyamandlovu. The cooperative does market gardening. For some, it has proven to be the best thing to happen to them. Those who join the co-op may stay for a three-month trial period; they then decide to stay (for a small fee) or move on.

The Zimbabwe Christian Mission welcomes others. This church body purchased a farm on which old people may opt for a renewed chance for normal life. Those who are able, work the land. Plans are underway to sink a borehole (to bore an Artesian well) to promote a better yield in market gardening. Some spend the day reviving former skills, like basket or mat weaving. Above all, the old people visit with each other. They share experiences. They provide companionship for each other—a healing balm to a broken spirit. In effect they say: ". . . we are not lost to society. We are people, and we matter. Our lives can be useful."

Unfortunately, some of the residents are never completely rehabilitated. A number go back to the street. For them, there is no better life than that of a wanderer. They might change cities, but they go on roaming as before. Streets will never be completely cleared, but efforts described here have improved some circumstances that seemed hopeless.

A number of shop owners in the railway station area do not help the situation. They have kept some people on the streets by subtle exploitation. They pay beggars a small amount to serve as night guards at shop entrances. These few spend their days on begging ventures in the city centre. Their nights are spent in makeshift, cardboard shelters, huddled in threadbare blankets at a shop entrance. Shop owners, meanwhile, eat bountifully from full tables and sleep in a snug, warm bed.

A portion of street people are ministered to under a special organization—EMTHUNZINI—also an outgrowth of the Mayor's call. This is headed by David Hdoda of the Salvation Army. This venture aims to rescue abused street children who are found selling or begging in the city centre. This operation is often hampered by parents of these children who sacrifice their children's lives in exchange for a meagre income.

The future will see greater development in the Bulawayo Shelter. Early on, it was staffed by three—a warden, a cook, and her assistant. Volunteers from different denominations help in varied ways; they also compose the Administrative Committee chaired by Richard Wilde of the Methodist Centre.

All funding is from local sources. Ninety-five percent comes from individual donors—in cash or kind—like the shoe factory owner who gave a truck load of offcuts (scraps or extra pieces) for use in shoe making and mending. Other groups also make generous donations. The Committee hopes that before long, the Bulawayo Shelter will be self-sufficient.

This endeavor would not have materialized if individuals like Inez Caldewood had failed to listen to the still small Voice. "To be continued" seems a worthy way to conclude.

14

Saudi Arabian Women at a Glance

Nirmala Nandakumar[*]

Anticipate an expression of what the author observed and experienced—honest, central feelings about cross-cultural encounter. Effective writing about and by women begins where women are. It reveals reality, including some more private realms. Traditional values, both cultural and religious, often do leave women vulnerable in the world. To tolerate another's sensitive critique lends integrity to hearing about cultural difference. A question to pose about male/female relationships, another's or our own, is: If authentic mutuality is not fostered, will individuals be limited?

Long ago, a great writer suggested something like, "Woman: thy name is patience." Or was it tolerance? Or might it better have been endurance? I found this composite of terms to be a most apt description of women of Saudi Arabia. Their tolerance, endurance, and patience are almost unbelievable.

---

[*]Nirmala Nandakumar is from Kerala, in south India. She is the mother of two adult children who attend United States graduate schools. From Saudi Arabia, she and her husband returned to India before living several years in Grenada. They recently moved to California.

My husband was in Saudi Arabia for six years, working as a doctor. I joined him for the last three years. This gave me opportunity to carefully observe women. Had I been able to speak and understand Arabic, I could have conversed with them. I could have understood their unique lifestyle better. I could have learned their view of cultural dimensions that appeared to me to enslave them. However, domination reaches far beyond the Middle East.

Many times I met women when they were not wearing their *burkhas*—for example, at the airport women's waiting lounge or the women's booth of the telephone exchange. Many of the women tried to be friendly, to start conversation. On such occasions, I felt frustrated because I was ignorant of their language.

Saudi women face basic, common problems. Distinct cultural features include a tradition of male domination and female subjection. In my view, the women of Saudi Arabia might be divided into two groups—the educated elite (often with royal or rich business linkage) and the nomadic Bedouins. The latter, more often illiterate, experience poor socioeconomic status. Less likely to know their rights, they remain more patient.

Difference in social status appears within school experience. Children of the elite often attend schools in France, the United Kingdom, or the United States. Girls enjoy their freedom. Some of them grow up as typical youth—wearing western dress or even acquiring a western accent. But for the daughters of the Bedouin, the very essence of being can be pathetic. Though they attend schools exclusively for girls, they never attend college.

When Bedouin girls reach the age of eleven or twelve, they must wear *Abhayas* or *burkhas*. Made of black synthetic material and stitched in a particular manner, this garment leaves only the hands and feet uncovered. A hood attached at the back of the neck covers the head and face. With some, a slit is neatly cut to make the eyes visible. In other cases, a translucent black piece of tunic is tied at the back of the head. This covers the entire head and countenance.

I can hardly imagine the effects of walking in such darkness. Many women do develop eye problems—mainly poor vision. During scorching summer months when temperatures can soar above fifty degrees celsius, their state is pitiful. But they tolerate the discomfort.

The black Bedouin women lead a nomadic life; they raise sheep. Some are hawkers, selling toiletries and jewelry near the hospital or *souk* (market). These women are independent and hard workers. They do not cover their face. On their pierced nose they wear large, colorful nose studs. They stain their hands heavily with henna (reddish-orange paste); their arms may be adorned with twenty to thirty tight, gold bangles. Quite tall and of solid build, they wear gaudy, long-sleeved, ankle-length frocks. Under this some wear a pair of tracksuit-type pants. Unfortunately, they appear unkempt and many are illiterate.

Stark comparison greets the beholder of beautiful, sophisticated Saudi women. Endowed with a flawless and fair complexion, they use a lot of make-up. They cover their delicate figures with skirts, pants, or long dresses. Further, they wear stiletto heels, have beautifully manicured hands, and anoint themselves with expensive perfumes.

Beautiful Saudi Arabian women have long and lustrous hair. But, since the Koran stipulates that a woman's face must not be visible to males, only her husband sees it. The same source suggests that hair is a woman's ornament that entices men. Hence, it should be covered. We foreign women also must wear the *Abhaya* and cover our hair whenever we go to the *souk* (market).

Two nurses from the local hospital visited my home. They first made certain that no men were in the house. When they removed their *burkhas*, I was astonished to see their beautiful faces. One had hair that extended to her knees. These women refused to be photographed, quoting the Koran as their reason. They were quite educated and spoke good English. In the hospital my husband recognizes them either by their voice or the color of the shoes they wear.

Arranged marriage is a gamble for many girls of Saudi Arabia. The bride first sees the groom on their wedding night. Young girls aged fourteen or fifteen often marry a man aged fifty or sixty. She may be his sixth, seventh, or even tenth wife. A young girl, traded by her father to marry an old man, may end up having a relationship with the husband's first wife's son. Closer in age to her, he more likely satisfies her needs and interests.

While in Saudi Arabia, I observed the plight of some wives. One wife of our houseowner, who was in his late seventies, stayed near our house. At first, I thought that she was his daughter. When my husband attended her seventh delivery, I learned that she was one of the man's four wives. While pregnant women may appear young under their *burkhas*, women doctors tell of encountering women in their late fifties who come to them for antenatal check-ups or to seek help for labor.

Polygamy is not practiced among Saudi's elite. But multiple pregnancies or illicit relations and adultery leave genetic and other effects, as is true worldwide. The average number of children among Saudi non-elites is rarely less than ten. A woman used primarily to produce babies must comply with her husband's wishes, even if her health is not good. Otherwise, she risks being repudiated. Also, a woman who does not become pregnant or bear a male child can be divorced.

Among Islamic people marriage is a civil contract. Customs of divorce (to give *talaq*) vary. In the process, a husband utters *talaq* three times in the woman's presence. *Iddat*, a cooling-off period, follows in which he can revoke the divorce. Many divorced women live in Saudi.

These may remarry, except for divorcees of the royal family. In the capital city of Riyadh, I saw many palatial mansions that belong to former wives of the King.

If a man chooses a fifth wife, he will divorce one of his other four, based on some judgment. While the sacred Koran declares this practice valid, not all Muslims choose the custom. Even so, for an Arab the Koran is not just a holy book to be carefully followed. That it is a way of life deserves explanation in a further article.

One common feature that I noticed about many Saudi Arabian women is ignorance about the outside world. Oblivious of a religion or faith other than Islam and with minimal general knowledge, such ignorance seems most unfortunate, to me. It seems to contradict other wealthy or technically-developed dimensions of Saudi Arabia.

I recall an incident while waiting at the King Abdul Aziz International Airport at Riyadh for my flight to Bombay. In the departure lounge, I sat next to a veiled but richly attired and strongly perfumed Saudi woman. She was curious about my mode of dress—my *sari*—plus the red dot on my forehead (essential for a Hindu married woman). She was going to Paris with her husband for a holiday. She could understand little that I tried to convey, although she was an educated Saudi who spoke fluent English.

She asked about my destination. When I responded "Bombay," she asked whether Bombay was in France or the United States. She had not heard of a country called India. While such lack of information could show up in other global airports, I thought, "So much for knowledge and education." Many Arab men likely prefer such isolation; many want their wives to be heavily veiled and in a "prison" of ignorance.

How I wish that *all* Saudi women could breathe the air of freedom to know the world beyond Saudi Arabia. Is that asking too much, when their menfolk have considerable freedom? Is ignorance to be tolerated? Does endurance within rigid restrictions contribute to human good will? Might the practice of patience unduly delay needed progress for the twenty-first century?

Any cross-cultural glance identifies but segments of the experience of national women. While the privilege has been mine to interact with Saudi Arabian women, the international community need not deny certain circumstances or practice. At the same time my intent has been to accurately inform, based on my experience. I long for human dignity and rights for all peoples. And women within Saudi Arabia who do not know privilege deserve our support with any effort to broaden that base among other women in their homeland.

Memories of incidents in Saudi Arabia of women's tolerance, patience, and endurance lingered, as I readjusted to my native India before moving next to Grenada.

15

Two Vignettes and a Story
Sonia Bai, "Rachel," and Dr. Yu Enmei

*Harriet Lapp Burkholder**

Anticipate hearing about women's conscious perceptions of their basic reality. Situate the specifics of each one's circumstance and how she adapted to or shaped her context. Observe survival skills, courage, and strength.

A Glimpse of Sonai Bai—Tucked away in a picturesque village of central India lived Sonai Bai—pastor's wife, trained nurse, mother and friend. I knew her in the 1920s when I was six to twelve years old.

The village of Ghatula was forty miles from Dhamtari, a good-sized town. To go between the two places entailed crossing two large rivers. When these rivers flooded during the rainy season of June through August, nearby residents were stranded. Low hills surrounded the area; a jungle loomed near. At night we could hear the occasional roar of a tiger or the munching of a bear on fruit called "Moha." This same fruit fell from a tree into my sandbox.

Into that isolated jungle setting Pastor Mukut Bhelwa took his young bride, a beautiful, refined, well-educated woman. Tragedy had left

*Harriet Lapp Burkholder lived her first eighteen years in India. She has enjoyed several visits to China, in addition to having lived there two years. The mother of four children (one adult son died), she is the wife of a retired pastor and college president.

her orphaned at a very early age. From the orphanage opened for famine victims and rejected children, she later trained in Mennonite mission schools.

Sonai Bai ("Bai" is a respectful phrase given to women of status) opened a clinic in Ghatula, a medically deprived area. From miles around, non-Christian people came to trust, respect, and love this woman of faith. For a woman to have formal education in this more remote Indian place, in the 1920s, was very unusual. For a woman to attend to male patients was also uncommon.

Sonai Bai was not alone in her work. With a year of medical school, my father joined her to perform minor surgeries. I often sat at the outside window to watch; I thought I wanted to pursue medicine. Severe cases were taken to the hospital in Dhamtari—the "ambulance" was a bed carried by family and friends.

I have distinct memories of Sonai Bai and Pastor Mukut's happy, supportive relationship. One sign of this was their walking side-by-side to church. Custom stipulated that a woman walk a few steps behind her husband. Already as a very young girl, I sensed delight in their model of mutuality. My best friend and playmate, during my three months at home from boarding school in the mountains, was their daughter Violet.

Sonai Bai became my childhood role model—a competent, courageous nurse; a compassionate friend, loving mother, and devoted wife. As a Christian, her deep faith impressed me.

Rachel *—Little did we know, as Rachel waved goodbye from the pier in Shanghai in 1949, what was in store for our friend. Because she had been employed by Church World Service, a United States organization, she was judged by Communist Party members to be guilty of being a spy or American collaborator. Although she had turned over all CWS money and property to the new Communist Party, she was imprisoned for two years and there knew harsh treatment.

A Christian, Rachel had been trained in Christian schools. Her husband, a Party member, was not a Christian. When offered a higher position if he would divorce Rachel, he refused. Not promoted, he was then located where Rachel could join him. She found only menial, low-paying jobs. They became parents of a daughter.

After so-called liberation in 1949, life was more settled in the block of years that followed. This period of calm was rudely interrupted in 1966 by the young Red Guards of the Cultural Revolution who tended to be ruthless and cruel. Rachel was removed from her teaching career in Peking (now Beijing), where her husband had a government position as an officer in the air force. Their crime this time: they were part of a growing elite professional group, not peasants. Both were sent to separate work-farms in the country. Occasional, brief visits followed.

On the work-farm, a woman who was positioned above Rachel treated her rudely. "But," she said, "I never forgot that, as a Christian, love must govern my attitudes and actions." This attitude helped. Ever since her early imprisonment, she had not attended a church, underground or government-approved.

After Rachel was released from work-camp and employed again, she went to see that same woman. She should not have gone, according to Chinese protocol. Because this woman was her superior in age and position, she should have waited until the woman came to her. But having been secretive about her Christian ideals, Rachel wanted to tell the woman that she forgave her. She hoped they could be friends.

As Rachel told us this several years ago in private, when a free woman, she burst into tears and said, "I hope God will forgive me, for having been a secret believer these past years, for not openly declaring my faith." She had never joined the Party either.

---

*Not actual name, to protect her identity.

Her story could be echoed by many during those same years in China. James, a church leader, also wept as he recalled how he and other Christians had burned their Bibles and Christian literature to hide their faith. "I hope God will forgive us!" he cried. Memories surfaced of the school building where he had been imprisoned: with only sloping desks to sleep on, and his family not allowed to bring him food.

So, what do we say to people like Rachel and James? How might we respond in the event of extensive political chaos and cruelty? Remembering my Anabaptist forebears who were tortured and killed for open, professed faith, I cannot judge people who suffer deeply. God knows all hearts and intents. From Rachel I learned that tragedy can come through a national situation, but that triumph can result from abiding faith.

Dr. Yu Enmei—Dr. Yu Enmei's story of twenty-seven years of imprisonment (1951 to 1978) reveals her deep Christian faith. She had been free for only a year when we first met in Chengdu, China. For the details of her story, I am indebted to a manuscript by Dorothy McCammon* based on interviews she had taped with Dr. Enmei.

Daughter of an Anglican rector, Yu Enmei's life began in a home that valued both the Gospel and education. For girls to attend college, plus medical school, was fairly unusual in China then. Shanghai, where she studied at Women's Medical College, is on the east coast of China. After training, she went west to Chungking to work in the Methodist Hospital. There she met Mennonite workers Don and Dorothy McCammon. While at that hospital, she was arrested.

Dr. Enmei came under suspicion because she had American friends with whom she kept in touch. Americans were enemies of Communists at that time. Enmei was also suspect because she had been abroad and was well-educated.

On the day Dr. Enmei was arrested, she was told that she would be giving a lecture. The jeep that transported her was curtained; she could not look out, and no one could see in. Taken to an unknown, up-

---

*More recently Harriet edited this, titled *Tragedy and Triumph, Courage and Faith Through 27 Years in Chinese Prisons*, San Francisco:Purple Bamboo Pub., 1993.

stairs room, her apartment keys were taken from her. While some people searched her apartment, others interrogated her. Asked about Olin Stockwell, a Methodist missionary acquaintance of hers already in jail, she was warned about refusing to cooperate: "I would hate to tell you the consequences," her interrogator threatened. Knowing her situation to be serious, she cited her habits as a loyal citizen. She wished only to serve the country; she had never had political discussions with Stockwell.

From there, Dr. Enmei was taken to a room where a woman searched her. She removed her watch, eyeglasses, and even her hairpins. Very near-sighted, the loss of glasses was crucial. Soon a man told her to follow him.

"It was an endless descent—steps, steps, steps down—like I was going to the end of the earth. When we finally stopped, he had this big key which opened a small, dark, heavy door. All was totally dark. I couldn't see anything. It was like a cavern. Then he opened another door and said 'You go in.' I knew I was in prison. I had nothing with me, but I was calm. I thought 'the worst has happened.' I was naive."

Naivete was the first stage of thought during Dr. Enmei's imprisonment. She believed that perhaps her profession as a doctor in a service situation would save her. Then came a second stage—*confusion*.

"I could not imagine what I was facing. I was confused. I asked myself, 'Why, why, why?' over and over. Since they had taken everything, they must not respect my profession."

Dr. Enmei's living conditions were stark. Her totally dark cell was almost the length of her height. Her food, black corn bread, was thrown to her through a hole in the door. She was often called for interrogation. Weakened from lack of food, she could scarcely climb the steps. Hand-cuffed during these sessions, she heard threats: a woman had been shot. Officials asked more about Olin Stockwell.

Dr. Enmei learned to change her tactics, to try to outwit her interrogators. Instead of giving negative answers, she suggested they give her time to think. She was given paper and pen to write her thoughts.

"I would write such foolish things," she said. "I would make up a lot of conversations that actually didn't take place."

She spent six months in that cell. Mud floor. At first no bedding or change of clothing. Her bathroom a bucket. Her daily trips up two flights of steps, to empty her bucket, provided her with some light and fresh air.

"I had a little fresh air. I enjoyed it. I saw light. To this day, light conveys a special sense of relief to me. The hymn 'Lead Kindly Light' came to mind; I often sang that in my later years. Later on, I also prayed for nothing but a little light."

How Dr. Enmei lived through those first months reflects special strength. Her faith, her will to live, and her hope that she would be released soon sustained her. At one point a young girl was placed in her room. She was delighted to have someone to talk to. However, she discovered that the girl was a spy.

After six months she was moved to a larger prison, into a room with twenty other inmates. That was the second largest prison in Chungking, called "the Stone Prison." Her roommates were opium addicts and prostitutes. She was the only political prisoner. Due to that, she was treated with disdain by the others. Conditions here were better; she was on first floor, plus she received a little more food. She had a plank for a bed and a stool on which to sit.

Dr. Enmei was eventually asked to help with clinical work, and still later to assist one of two doctors. Because she had been kind to prisoners, they chose to go to the doctor she was helping rather than the other man. This made the latter very jealous. It also added misery to Enmei's life.

She became depressed; she questioned her faith. When she attempted suicide by jumping into a pool, other inmates saved her. For doing that, she was given severe punishment in solitary confinement. She then recalled an incident when as a child, she fell into a well. When she was rescued, her father assured her that her life had a distinct purpose. That memory served as a turning point for her weakened faith while in prison. With renewed awareness of God's purpose, she handled what happened to her with new strength. *Renewed faith* marked her third stage of thought.

In 1956, five years after the first imprisonment, she was moved to prison number three. Although she had known some kindness along the way, being a political prisoner left her far from free. She was moved to an agricultural prison farm, in hilly country south of Chengdu. Here she gained some status when she was asked to train people to be medical assistants. Housed with the cadres and eating with them improved life for her.

However, two events made the situation worse. First, in 1960, a three-year famine began. Food became scarce. Second, and worse, 1966 brought the Cultural Revolution. Dr. Enmei was interrogated in front of a group of cadres. Once more she was consigned to darkness and solitary because she was a professional person, not a peasant. This lasted for nineteen months. (Millions of intellectuals were killed during the Cultural Revolution; the whole story of that ten-year period has never been told.)

Finally in 1972, Enmei was moved to an Agriculture Research Center where her living situation definitely improved. Her possessions, which had been taken from her apartment in 1951, were returned. Her books had become moldy. By this time she had reached the fourth stage of thought—*resignation*.

"The worst they can do is kill me. And if I'm killed, so what. If I live, okay, and if I die, okay. An acceptance of the worst lingered." After a serious, self-diagnosed illness—pulmonary embolism—she was moved to the camp hospital and finally on to freedom in Chengdu.

For some years after her release, Dr. Enmei continued to serve her country, the country she loves. She believed with all her heart that she had work to do, as long as she was mentally and physically fit. She was intentional to let her "light"—that most important metaphor—illumine the way.

[Editor's Postscript: The following excerpts are adapted from a brief article by Anna Juhnke which appeared in the Oct/Nov 1988 issue of *Window to Mission*.]

Dr. Yu Enmei's bravery continues. Not only did she rescue wounded people between Japanese bombing attacks on Chungking during World War II. Not only did she endure twenty-seven years of prison and labor reform camps. After her release, she founded a training center for parents and teachers involved with mentally handicapped children.

Her name has been cleared by the Chinese government. And her province has named her to the Standing Committee of the People's Consultative Committee. This group hears and comments on proposed legislation for the province and country. She has assisted with moral education through a radio school and has given health lectures for the elderly or for the Child Welfare Institute. Her courage and joyful commitment continued.

16

Djiboutian Women
and the Story of "Saida"

*Marian Hostetler**

> *Anticipate attitudes, values, and meanings and note how they are revealed. Forces in a person's social setting— such as traditional family patterns—can leave women unprepared for the larger world. Be alert to the Djiboutian women's perceptions of their choices or the risks they face.*

I will share a few facts I have learned from observing Djiboutian (ji-boosh'-n) women for several years. A glimpse into one woman's story then follows.

General Background—Djibouti (ji-boot'-ee) is a small country in the Horn of Africa. A former French colony previously known as French Somaliland and later as the Territory of the Afars and the Issas, Djibouti has been an independent country since 1977. (See map at front of book.)

While the people's nationality is Djiboutian, actually, no ethnic

---

*Marian Hostetler's several-year assignment with Eastern Mennonite Board of Missions in Djibouti began in 1989. She has also lived in the African countries of Algeria, Chad, Cote d-Ivoire, Benin, and Somalia. Her published books include: *African Adventure, Journey to Jerusalem, Fear in Algeria, Secret in the City, Mystery at the Mall, They Loved their Enemies*, and *We Knew Paul.*

Djiboutian people exist. They are ethnically either Afars (a group diffused from Ethiopia into Djibouti) or Issas (a Somali tribe). Some are also Arabs, originally from nearby Yemen. Djiboutians are multilingual, using their native languages at home. Courses in school begin in French, then include Arabic; later English might be learned. Most people are Muslim. Christianity is present only among foreigners from France, Ethiopia, and elsewhere.

Most Djiboutians do not read or write. According to a recent European Economic Community report, ninety-one percent of women and eighty-five percent of men here are illiterate.

Another cultural fact is that young girls undergo female circumcision. There are three forms of this, from mild to severe. The present trend is toward a milder form, rather than eliminating the practice altogether. Women endure a re-operation after marriage, in order to have sexual relations.

Dress—Features of dress vary. Although many Djiboutians are Muslim, most women are not veiled. Those women occasionally seen veiled are foreigners. Some Djiboutians, mainly of Arabic origin, wear a white scarf wound around the head and a long black robe over their other clothing. Girls and students wear western-style clothes.

The usual street and office style of dress for women, the *diiric*, is both attractive and unique to this area of Africa. These dresses are long, made of one piece of folded cloth. The snipped-out neck area plus the bottom are hemmed, each side has a full seam, leaving holes near the top for the arms.

Under this *diiric* a slip is worn. Plain but color-coordinated with the print dress, it includes fancy embroidery work. The dress is always pulled up—usually held in place by the elbow or else tucked into the waist of the slip—so that the slip is visible. The *diiric* forms an integral part of the outfit. Over the shoulders (and sometimes over the head) is a matching colored scarf or shawl. Everyday wear, or the outfits of poor people, are of poorer quality and less well-matched, but of similar style.

Monetary Matters—Djibouti is poor, without natural resources. Even so, the many approaches women utilize to earn money impresses me. Outside the school where I teach, thirty to fifty women regularly gather to sell snacks to students between classes. They bring their "shops" with them via wheelbarrows, shopping carts, or old baby carriages. Some have large thermoses or coolers for dispensing sodas. Others provide homemade popsicles, triple-flavored ice cream on sticks, or frozen juice in plastic baggies. With the latter, the buyer bites off a corner and sucks out the juice as it melts.

Other income options exist. Some women manage mini-restaurants. Their clients sit on empty powdered-milk cans. Some sell candies and/or baked or deep-fried cakes and rolls. Some set up beach umbrellas (often made by cigarette companies for advertising) for shade. Others crouch in the meager shade of walls, moving as the day progresses and the shaded area shifts. For still others, a piece of paper serves two purposes—to provide shade and chase flies, as needed.

Along one street in the city, seated on the curb, are the women I call the "watch ladies." Twenty of them dangle watches and a few necklaces from their fingers. No doubt, each one has her allotted foot of space in which to sell.

Both women and men work with sewing machines. They and

their treadle machines dot the scenery in some areas. They wait for customers who have just visited one of the fabric shops to bring business. One sewed a *diiric* and slip for me in fifteen minutes!

Hours of official work day vary. Banks and government offices are open from 7:30 in the morning to 1:00 or 1:30 in the afternoon. Schools run from 7:30 to 11:30 and 3:30 to 6:30. Everything is closed during the heat of the day. At 4:30 or 5:00 shops and markets then re-open.

Beggars—young girls, mothers with babies, old women, and men—linger near their favorite haunts: banks, the post office, and every bus stop. How to respond to their constant calls—*baksheesh, baksheesh* (money)—is a recurring question. No one procedure satisfies me.

One solution, hinted at in one of my books, *African Adventure*, raises a probing question. A foreign girl asks her mother if more good might have resulted from their sponsoring agency's having sent money for the poor instead of sending them to work there. Perhaps, however, the workers were needed to help eliminate the causes of poverty and hunger.

Another approach might be to regard the beggars as other merchants. For many, begging is a chosen way to earn a living. Just as no one contributes to all merchants, so with beggars. Attitude shapes approach. Sometimes I resent a beggar's persistence or doubt the person's actual need. A further, debatable, response states, "*Ilaahay ha nasiiyo*" which in Somali means, "God will provide."

As I learn more language, I hope to enter into conversation with some beggars who approach me. Instead of ignoring them, I prefer to recognize them as persons. For the present, each encounter calls for a decision, whether to look the other way, give a small coin, or offer a piece of food (as on leaving a grocery store).

An unhealthy source of income comes from the sale of the drug *khat*. Six tons of this drug enter daily into Djibouti from Ethiopia. It causes Djibouti's biggest social problem. The green leaves of the plant contain a substance similar to that found in amphetamines. It can be both a stimulant and a depressant. People pull off the two-inch leaves and chew them like tobacco. This causes their cheeks to bulge; when their mouth opens, green saliva and gums appear. Ninety percent of the men sit all afternoon with their friends and chew *khat*. They spend money for this rather than for family needs.

Colonizers are known to have introduced *khat*. It left people lethargic or more easy to handle. Chewing also fosters tribalism, as those of "one's own kind" sit together to munch and talk. Government attempts to get rid of *khat* have failed. Newspaper mottos like: "Drivers! Don't use *khat* or alcohol when driving" have not changed patterns among bus or taxi drivers.

However, few women chew *khat*. Why not more? Recently, a visiting professor and expert in Somali culture and history reported that Djiboutian men are opposed to women chewing it. Men told him that if women became *khat* chewers, everything in Djibouti would come to a halt. Women, the more active and assertive ones, keep things moving. That's true for even the sale of *khat*! The women need only some boards nailed together for a table and a burlap bag to keep the product fresh and protected.

Specific Customs—Djiboutian women like to celebrate. A boss of a small crew of women who are house-helpers for foreigners invited many people to her *afartaan bixi*. That means the forty-day coming-out party. After visiting her husband who works in Saudi Arabia, she had returned pregnant. When her son was born, both she and the child were housebound for forty days, as is the custom.

Then came the big party. About a hundred people crowded into two rooms. Women's gold and silver embroidered dresses sparkled as they sang and danced to the beat of tambourine and drum. The video camera rolled. Poems were recited in honor of the new son. There was food for everyone. The baby, outfitted in sweater, knit panties and booties in spite of 100 degree temperature, slept through it all.

Nearly half of the students in my secondary English classes (freshman and sophomore level) are girls. As with students everywhere, they vary in size—tall, short and stocky. Their interest in classwork ranges from strong to couldn't-care-less. They appear in conservative Muslim, Djiboutian *diiric*, or western modern dress.

What's ahead for these girls? Consider Samira's circumstance. A student I had first known in Somalia, Samira was a bit older than these ninth and tenth grade Djiboutians. When I asked students to write about a childhood memory, she wrote:

"When I was a child, I experienced many things. My father divorced my mother when I was three years old and my sister was two. My mother went to our country where she married again. My father didn't get married; he took care of us. When I was seven my father died. My younger sister couldn't do anything. We were alone and without much money. One of my father's best friends heard that he had died. This man took us to his house. We were there for about ten years; we lived a happy life."

Samira, whose name means "patience," is appropriately named.

Saida, an Example—The woman I learned to know best is not a typical Djiboutian. In fact, she was a refugee from Somalia. She had fled to Djibouti when her city of Hargeisa was destroyed by government troops fighting rebel troops.

Saida (fictitious name) spoke Somali, Arabic, English, and German fluently. She had been educated in Saudi Arabia, England, and Germany as well as in Somalia. She had been a teacher, wife, and mother. About ten years earlier her husband left her. He later divorced her and married another woman. He abandoned Saida, leaving her to raise their two daughters alone, except for some unwanted interference from his mother and brothers.

When I knew Saida, her daughters were twelve and nineteen. I never met them or saw where she lived. She protected her privacy. Perhaps because she lived in poor circumstances or because she did not want foreigners in her neighborhood, she never told us where she lived.

My colleague Cindy and I first met Saida one spring. Another mission group had learned to know her and hired her as a teaching aide for a Somali language course with their workers. Cindy and I both wanted a language tutor, so we were introduced to Saida. She came to my apartment twice a week, and to Cindy's three times a week.

Saida was a tall, pleasant-looking woman. Her smile revealed a characteristic of many Somalis—prominent front teeth with a gap between the two top middle ones. She wore typical local dress. When entering the apartment, she left her thongs at the door and took off the shawl draped over her head. Her hair remained covered with a scarf.

She was a gracious, strong, and friendly person. She had some knowledge of Christianity from travels, studies, and association with other missions. When we talked about frankincense and myrrh—native trees and widely-used spices in this area—we looked at the Matthew passage in my Arabic Bible where these were given to Jesus. She later gave me a gift of a Somali incense burner and charcoal, plus some of these two spices to burn.

Saida was a knowledgeable teacher, effective with difficult explanations. She understood Somali grammar and was quick to share Somali proverbs, sayings, and cultural practices. Since she knew English so well, we easily relied on that. This meant that I learned less Somali.

Suddenly Saida did not come to teach. We had no way to contact her. We only heard of some difficulty with her former husband. Several weeks later she reappeared. Her former husband had said he would come from his work in Saudi Arabia during Ramadan—the Muslim month of fasting. So she had stayed home, but he never arrived. The purpose of his proposed visit was to arrange the marriage of their daughter with a Djiboutian acquaintance of his. He sent a wealthy Djiboutian friend to act as his intermediary to begin arrangements.

Saida and her daughter opposed this plan. She was very upset. Tears came to her eyes as she talked about it. Why would he do this? Why should he interfere now? Would he be able to force this marriage? He had friends and influence; she had nothing. All she could do was pray to God.

Then one day she announced that she had sent her daughter to Aden (in Yemen) where she had family members. How or where they managed to find the money for this, I do not know. We continued our Somali lessons for a while. One day Cindy received an unexpected phone call from Saida—from Aden. She had gone there too.

Since then, we have had no word. If she leaves Aden, she will probably return to Hargeisa, her home town. Although she no longer teaches us language or details of culture, she remains in my thoughts, memory, and prayers.

17

"Anna": Soviet Woman on a Tight Rope

Margaret Sawatsky[*]

> *Anticipate the dilemma of prescribed sex roles and the process entailed when women reflect on their choices. Has religious blessing of the social order thwarted women in most global settings? What do we learn from the intersection of fictitious and real life?*
>
> *Keep in mind that while the terms Soviet or Soviet Union are no longer in use—they were when the author first knew Anna (whose name here has been changed).*

I. Anna—I would like you to meet Anna, a Russian Mennonite woman. She represents the many women in that country who struggle to survive, who struggle to balance two poles. Russia: a country that idealizes women and gives awards to mothers with large families. Russia: in reality, a land where daily existence for women can be very harsh.

Anna is among the ninety-two percent of all working-age women who work outside the home. Often, in addition to forty-two hours of

---

[*]Margaret Sawatsky lived in Europe from 1973-1985. In addition to four trips into Russia, she has known Russian immigrants living in Germany. Earlier a mental health worker and chaplain in Canada, she continues as a mental health worker in Elkhart, Indiana, while completing a degree at Associated Mennonite Biblical Seminary.

employment per week, she works fifty more hours at home. She carries a net bag with her at all times. After work, she might shop. That involves standing in line for hours for basic groceries, and then sometimes being rudely told that supplies are sold out.

Housework stretches out, too. Anna is fortunate to have a few chickens and a pig which provide protein for the family. All household chores—cooking, sewing, washing clothes—are socialized to be "women's work." When the children are sick, Anna is responsible for their care. Her work is never done.

Twice during the week, plus twice on Sunday, Anna goes to church. Neighbors and work colleagues sometimes laugh at her naive faith in God, her simple outlook on life. Sometimes they are even hostile. How do women like Anna survive, with their faith, health, and families intact?

I first met Anna in 1977 at Alma Ata, Soviet Union. Her family had tried unsuccessfully for ten years to emigrate to West Germany. One daughter, already there, had recently given birth to a severely handicapped baby. That caused her a nearly-complete emotional breakdown. A son of Anna's had just been exiled to Eastern Siberia for five years. The sentence, for accidentally killing a pedestrian, was harsh. There was speculation about whether the fact that he was a Christian and ethnically German had shaped the outcome of the trial. Two of Anna's children remained at home.

Anna herself suffered from various physical problems common among women her age. Her husband also was not well. He was said to be suffering from "nerve" problems. He had difficulty completing unskilled labor.

Anna, ethnically German but living in the Soviet Union, is of the minority Mennonite faith. She lives out her faith through complete devotion to her family. For her, living for Christ means literally to give her total self at all times. This gives meaning and fulfillment to her life. She receives spiritual and emotional support from the church where she pours out her heart during prayer time. While her hope is to be ever faithful, above all, she prays for permission to emigrate with her family to West Germany, the "Promised Land."

II. Beyond Anna, Comparisons in Literature—How representative was Anna's life of women in the Soviet Union?

Whenever I traveled in that region, I was told that under Soviet socialism full equality between the sexes had been achieved. Women were emancipated. Further, images of Soviet women conveyed in the west depicted those who successfully combined chosen careers with competent motherhood. But I always wondered.

Both scholarly studies and fiction provide extensive data to show that not all has been well. Lynne Attwood's book *The New Soviet Man and Woman*, (Indiana University Press, 1990), shatters the myth hailed as the big achievement of the 1917 Revolution—equality of the sexes. Whereas Soviet law implies that men and women have equal rights, gender stereotypes persist, reinforced in recent decades.

Russia's patriarchal system has survived since prerevolutionary times. Pushed underground briefly, it rebounded since 1960 when flaws in socialist society became more evident. Attention turned to one of the most significant developments in the Soviet Union—the employment of women. "It was bound to come under scrutiny as one of the possible causes of lingering social problems," Attwood writes.

In his 1987 book on *perestroika*, former leader Gorbachev himself stated that problems in society stem from the "weakening of family ties and slack family responsibilities." He preferred that women reduce their work load outside the home so that they have more time for "domestic duties." They could return to their "purely womanly mission."

The portrayal of women succeeding in careers while being devoted wives and mothers is rarely true to Soviet reality, says Attwood. Women must choose to put either work or family first. Further, Soviet press articles make frequent charges against women. Stolin, a journalist, says, "[W]omen who attempt to divide themselves between family and work put themselves into an intolerable psychological position—the result of which is guilt." Attwood's analysis of family erosion and birthrate decline are linked to the strong work orientation encouraged for women. This led to a reappraisal of gender roles and a call to return to more traditional family roles.

With the myth of feminine liberation in the Soviet Union shattered, and the entire Soviet system collapsed, readers will wonder what direction the commonwealth of Russia will take. What will life be like for a woman in the 1990s who lives in the territories of what was once the Soviet Union?

A popular 1989 book of nineteen contemporary short stories written by Russian women describes daily life as walking a tight rope. Titled *Balancing Acts*, this rich anthology stimulates awareness of and appreciation for the modern Russian woman's "self perception in literary form."

The sampling includes rural and urban settings, feminist and traditionalist thought. War experience recurs. Stories paint a bleak picture of disintegrated family ties, daily indignities, and an absence of security. To counter this, some writers reflect a drive for personal and professional fulfillment. Others succumb to the emotional pain of working to balance career with the role of wife and mother.

The main character, Tenechka, in "A Business Trip Home," forfeits maternal rewards in order to further her career. Tenechka, an archeologist, knows pain in balancing her professional life and mothering. Away from her son whom she leaves with her parents, she tries to be a mother when she returns. After he has turned twelve, she realizes that he is growing away from her. Aware that "we give people back what we get from them," (p. 70) she admits that her son has little to give her.

The main character in the story, "Peters," did not succeed in the world. "I'm talking about life, and how it always teases us, showing us and then taking away, showing and taking. You know, it's like a show window, all shiny and locked up tight, and you can't get anything out of it." (p. 23)

The primacy of motherhood becomes the central theme in "The Road to Aktanysh."

> All her life she had aimed at something that she thought
> was happiness, and she had thrust aside the most impor-
> tant thing . . . whatever you accomplished you couldn't
> be content until you fulfilled the most important law.
> The law of continuation of the species. The Law of Life!
> (p. 399)

In "Home," the parents sacrifice everything for their daughter only to have lost something much greater. It "had disappeared unnoticed, and now was irretrievable." (p. 284)

The daughter in "Between Spring and Summer" asks for only one thing: "let me live my own life." (p. 343) But the parents say, "we don't have time to read or think . . . we live for our children." The father is convinced that the woman runs the household.

> Kenia (wife/mother) was the head of the house. She was the one who made all decisions . . . Why should they obey and respect a husband if he was a blank space around the house and couldn't even hammer a nail . . . Equal rights were good—our big achievement. But raising kids without fathers—a disaster. (p. 364)

Like many other men, his father had been killed during the war, leaving his mother to raise the kids alone. "Sons who are obedient to mothers, become obedient husbands," the husband concludes.

As is true of the majority of women writers in Russia today, these professional authors reveal their inner world in minute detail. They sensitively portray everyday, frantic, life and explore the drive for personal/professional fulfillment. They expose the deep emotional pain of living in such family settings. Nothing is hidden or sacred.

III. Anna, Reprieve?—In 1984, Anna's prayer was answered. Her family received permission to emigrate. For Anna, permission to leave the Soviet Union was clearly an indication that God had heard and answered her prayers. She arrived in Germany just when her daughter was trying to repair a broken marriage. That effort did, in fact, succeed. Anna's church in Germany also continues to thrive.

But I wonder about all the other Annas in the vast land of the Soviet Union. Will they, too, continue to live like Anna—waiting for a "Promised Land"? Will they find hope through, or in spite of, the tight rope? Are professional and domestic balancing acts realistic?

18

Toward Writing About a Friend
Mary Jean Yoder

Dorothy Yoder Nyce

Anticipate hearing a voice of authority through her private journal. Observe a person who, assured of her Escort, transformed gendered roles often implied in culture by taking her place in life with openness, humor, and courage.

"I cannot live without my macaroon!" For some odd reason that line from a college play has stuck with me for over thirty years. Yet, at other times, I can forget within minutes the name of a person just introduced. Attention is one factor; context and association may be others.

Why did the macaroon imagery stick? Who knows? Not an exercise in psychology, this article introduces you to a college friend—Mary Jean Yoder. Small in stature, with casual, blond hair and vibrant, blue eyes, Mary Jean combined spontaneous vim and vigor with serious depth.

For Mary Jean, life was real. Nevertheless, she enjoyed acting. To perform another's role expanded her expressive options. This demure, snippet of a young woman stood shouting on stage, "I cannot live without my macaroon!" It may have been the opening line, or one that recurred in the one-act production.

What then made the macaroon so essential? Why could the actor not live without it? Perhaps the expression hid a deeper desire. Perhaps it mimicked the trivial. Whether Mary Jean in life ever ate the small cookie made of egg white, sugar, and crushed almonds or coconut, I do not know. But few qualities about her proved to be trite.

Mary Jean lived a shorter life than most in our college and medical school classes. A couple weeks after being graduated from medical school with highest honors, she had a car accident. I think of her whenever I drive through the fatal intersection. Mary Jean died in 1964 at age twenty-five. To suggest that she did not live long enough is debatable. For she filled or shaped that quarter century with more than many people do in three.

I received the news of Mary Jean's death while teaching at Woodstock School in India. A child ran up to me asking why I had tears. "Well, Amy, a good friend of mine died. I can't imagine *any* Wisdom in that, but I'm trying to believe it. Do you remember that a friend visited me a couple months ago? Well, she isn't living anymore; she died after a car accident in the States. And my tears just roll down, because I liked her."

And then other memories surfaced. In a college dorm lounge, we had told each other that we would meet some day in India. And we had, just recently! Amazed at how quickly her Hindi returned, I knew she had learned it well. She approached everything with discipline. She could name wildflowers on the Himalayan hillside; she perfectly draped a sari; she paid the coolie for carrying her luggage more than was necessary because she "didn't want him to have less than enough."

Combining Mary Jean's diaries, journals, and letters with writings of her friends, a family acquaintance, Evelyn Bauer of Goshen, Indiana, prepared a manuscript about Mary Jean's life. Although the 150-page manuscript was never published, this article will lift quotes from it. These will be framed within themes that other writers about women (noted in the preface to this collection) find important to include.

Mary Jean cannot be interviewed. We cannot probe her mind about ideas in her journals. We cannot ask, "What did you mean by that?" So we must listen with care to her words and to words written about her. Having heard or read, we then interpret. As interpreters, we also must be careful, for our worldview may not comprehend hers. Although readers may be inspired by another woman's story, their own perceptions or choices determine the depth of understanding that follows.

Mary Jean's early years were lived in India. She attended Woodstock, a boarding school, most of her elementary years. High school and college years found her in Goshen, Indiana. The middle of three sisters, she loved family in distinct ways. Her physician father influenced her professional choice. While in medical school, her parents, Fyrne and Jonathan, worked in India and Nepal. Mary Jean's journal, therefore, moves between two worlds, being sometimes with her family, at other times writing to them twice a week. Discover Mary Jean, the fun-loving, disciplined subject of this account.

Qualities to note when beginning to describe a woman's strength or personal authority include: truthfulness, experience of friendship, her sense of hope and purpose, and achievements.

Mary Jean's journal discloses honesty, and *truthfulness*. Not hesitant to reveal her private self, she noted the following on different occasions:

> What a day! The thing that's made me feel all wrong was that chemistry test—Goodness. I really messed that up more than . . . God, help me so I won't think so much about grades.

> Didn't get as much done today as I wanted to but, tough, I never do.

> I'm happy inside me, really truly happy, but yet I'm confused . . . I think it's my future that confuses me . . . God knows; God guide!

Throughout her journal, Mary Jean sprinkles the phrase, "God Guide." Her petition reflects assurance. Not a distant deity, God was for her a true Companion. Ever constant, God's Presence was claimed as vital as breath. Not piety seeking public approval, her faith knew a Force or Energy within that walked or ran, laughed or cried along with her.

Occasions varied but her principles remained firm. Soon after beginning a term of voluntary service, Mary Jean wrote in all honesty, "Today was the second day at work and it was a long shift . . . I catch myself not liking to bathe, not liking to dress—because these activities are so closely connected with the girls I worked with today. By this time it all sort of repulses me. Forgive me, but that's the way it is right now."

During tough medical training she noted, "And it is really a SHAME that students entering an honest profession do the amount of cheating that our class does . . . It was the same last Tuesday on the Neurodiagnosis exam . . . Gets me a little cross."

In Puerto Rico for a short-term assignment, Mary Jean admitted, "Am finding two things as my primary problems. The biggest is the language . . . especially those verb tenses! I just don't know how I can jump that barrier in three months. The other thing is to really find a place where I can contribute. I hate to be given my board and room just to be a spectator."

A significant dimension of Mary Jean's strength was expressed through *friendship*. Not hesitant, she owned and expressed feelings. She gave reason for her attitudes and hinted about meanings behind thoughts. She shared her values without imposing them. Free verse frequents her journal, such as with this linking of both problems and joy with the *fun* of friendship.

> I remember you
> My friend.
> You listened with your heart
> To me,
> You had your problems too,
> Of course,
> And that was fun.
>
> I remember you,
> My friend.
> We were hilariously alive
> O'er hills,
> And bursting with a quiet joy,
> Free joy.
> And that was fun.

A friend reported the spice Mary Jean added: ". . . she was a great mimic and would entertain her friends with caricatures of other people." She demonstrated an uncanny distinction between making fun of another and providing humor because of keen observation that left her vulnerable, too.

Not afraid to express the kind of longing that grows with friendship, Mary Jean recorded: "I wish I could talk to Midge just now . . ." So also, in a letter to family members in India: "The evening is mild and pleasant. Wish I could share it with you, Mother and Ruth. There you are in the mildews! But, what I wouldn't give for the sight of the rising mists, the ferned trees, the reindeer orchids, and the happy sound of the rain on the tin roof!" Through conscious memory, she noted vivid details. Though separated by continents, expression offered a bond of knowing what others could see and hear in person.

A college roommate also saw how Mary Jean expressed friendship close at hand: "There were some honest and wholehearted arguments and sometimes bitter words. But the thing which impressed me, as a third party observing normal sisterly quarrels (often about borrowing clothes) was the forgiveness that invariably followed . . . The most important thing was not to avoid all conflict or disagreement . . . They also showed fierce loyalty."

Prone to reflect, Mary Jean wrote: "It's interesting, the way relationships go. Yet those of my family and others whom I know very well cannot be divided with the rest into a certain level of relationship. We seem to meet on many levels and this is what gives our friendship more depth. We know the minutes of each other as well as the decades. We see each others' lives in more distinct and deep perspective."

Effective writers about women keep alert to women's perceptions of their choices, noting how women feel about their range of responses. With a subject like Mary Jean, this is made easy. She kept her family in India informed of both plans and outcomes, as the following sequence depicts.

"We've been having a scheme growing for next year. We thought maybe we could rent a house and four of us med students and Lena could share it . . . I think we could get a house with upstairs, so that there could be some amount of privacy from the bustle of downstairs."

". . . Yes, I've been having plenty of good times too. Mother, you should be living with us. I really don't think I've laughed so much for a long time—at least in quantity."

"Marge just came in to talk to me . . . she thought my value system was a bit distorted—that I really hadn't been spending much time with (my housemates) . . . I really was glad that Marge felt free to tell me how she felt."

While a student, Mary Jean, on a purely volunteer basis, helped several high school girls with their more difficult school work . . . Her friendship grew with Rachel Cody, an African-American sophomore, living on her block. Years later, Rachel's respect and appreciation remains: "I got the impression she was friendly to anything that had life! . . . I still feel that she is a 'light' to my day . . . I shall always remember her telling me to 'never give up.'"

Several quotes reveal Mary Jean's clear sense of *purpose*. This had about it constancy, within different settings. How she ordered her thoughts also surfaced. During college, she wrote what she believed about God.

". . . there are basically two decisions which we must make. 1) Do I choose to believe God exists, or not? 2) If God exists, do I recognize or defy God? . . . Now, as a subject of God, my duty is to find out what God expects of me. What is God's purpose for and in me? . . . THERE-FORE I am not my own. I belong to God who has placed me here for a purpose."

Two further comments dovetail. Because of the first—"Time is one of my most precious things . . . every day is holy and all I do is a sacrament"—perspective for the second becomes clear. "Assisted at a vaginal hysterectomy on Thursday, combined with anterior-posterior repair for rectocele and cystocele. Holding retractors and cutting sutures isn't really glamorous, but I don't mind it at all . . . I started some i.v.'s, drew a lot of blood samples, changed dressings and irrigated abscesses, wrote up history/physicals, pulled some horrid boners which are best forgotten . . . and in general I've been sort of busy, a bit scared, but having fun."

Not knowing these would be her final New Year's resolutions, Mary Jean set forth these goals in January 1964.

1) make decisions in faith,
2) reserve one hour a day for Bible study and prayer,
3) write one letter per week, in addition to writing to family,
4) consider Bible classes for future training,
5) pray for Dad's job,
6) determine more definitely my basic life investment.

From early on, Mary Jean could be called an *achiever*. A classmate recalls that in grade school "she could run faster, climb better, yell louder, and be more daring than anyone else . . . Many of us asked her for advice, even at the ages of 10 and 11, because of her sureness."

A college friend noted: "She studied hard because she always had a goal for the future . . . she never seemed to lose sight of it." With perspective long-term or short, as "God, help that my speech might be all right tomorrow . . . ," Mary Jean chose for herself which experiences and feelings to keep centered.

To achieve meant for her not only to perform well, but also to finish. She struggled internally as an achiever with how much attention to give to grades. At one time she wrote: "My grades this term keep me in the upper 20 of the class . . . I'm trying to learn the stuff and to get this grades emphasis out of my worrying head." On another occasion: ". . . I want to be a good student . . . little 'blows' from not being at the top . . . teach me that I am not living this life in my own strength. It is my duty not to *strive* but to be open to the work that is to be done through me." When graduated at Indiana University, she placed 16th in her medical school class of 164 students. She had finished first in our Goshen College class of 250.

In the process toward becoming a doctor, Mary Jean used terms like "full force, strive, and highest." These characterized in part her direct social and work milieu. Always conscious of her setting, she helped shape it. A series of her quotes flesh out both her rigorous process (mixing hopes with fears) and achievement-oriented context.

"Well, we are really in it full force. About six hours a day in lab—with the cadaver."

". . . here I am in another of those sleepless nights that is making me wonder if I have the emotional make-up for this training . . . Our Radiographic final is tomorrow, Saturday is the final in Biophysics, Tuesday our final in Gross and Neuroanatomy lab, then Saturday our Neuro written final."

"They tell me the lecturer in Parasitology is very good. I do hope I enjoy that because I may have a bit greater need to learn in that field—important with tropical diseases."

"Pharmacology lab today was testing the action of tranquilizers and analgesics on the reflexes and general responses of a dog. We tested morphine, reserpine, and chlorpromazine."

"Let's see, when I wrote the last time, how many babies had I delivered? Well, now it's six . . . My ratio is five boys to one girl, and the heaviest one was 10 pounds and 6 ounces—which is quite a bundle . . .

I've really enjoyed this work."

"Oh, a little gem—the residents we work with voted three of us 'highest' in this class (40 of us) on OB-Gyn, and I was one."

Mary Jean was granted a scholarship from the Smith-Kline-French Foreign Fellowship for the summer of 1964 in Nepal. With congratulations from her classmates and professors, she began preparations. She told a nurse in Nepal, "It is such a challenge to make all the diagnoses one has to make here." That nurse later observed: "She spent much time reading in the library, looking up information relating to her cases."

In addition to a woman's qualities that shape her story, other features sharpen the composite. Components such as her relationships and cultural influences enter the scene. How she does theology makes a difference. Her virtues—whether of wit, will, or wisdom—as well as her feelings and attitudes, add to the narrative.

Women value *relationships*. Is that a stereotype? Does respect for the relational diminish expectations for logical or interdisciplinary thought? Or, if so, can that be countered? Women do need to avoid traditional biases that leave them vulnerable in today's world. But because women value being inter-dependent or practice greater mutuality need not foster their passivity.

When an older teen, she wrote the following about work as a summer waitress, on the Indiana Toll Road. "Today I worked at Bay 3. That's a pretty lousy place to get tips . . . Talked to Hazel a bit. She had her first child when she was 17 . . . She's married again now . . . an <u>awful</u> lot of these people I work with come from difficult home situations . . . We look for rewards. We move each plate hoping there'll be something under it. Dimes, nickels and even pennies really begin to mean something. We wonder what the others have gotten . . . The whole thing is so unpredictable, so minute, and yet really important to us each day."

As a college-age, summer volunteer at Woods, Mary Jean related with people with multi-handicaps: "Very few of the children have a mentality above 2-year olds. Many are also so physically handicapped . . . Many are seizure cases and unpredictably temperamental. Since I don't know all the kids' habits, my responses throw them 'off' . . . No, they weren't kidding when they told me that Annie F. is a real pill . . . And yet she seems to be really happy with a word or two of praise when she obeys."

Mary Jean also methodically processed questions about a marriage relationship: "I do believe that due to the culture I have inherited, due to the ideas that have been instilled in me, and due to the practices which have become familiar to me—as well as due to my emotional make-up—I don't believe I was carved out to hoe the row alone."

Further, she wrote, "I believe God wants me to work in partnership—as a 'helpmeet' to another. God will prosper my doctoring only in so far as it will give me the capacity to be a better <u>helper</u> to another." Her poetic self found voice:

> The first young blossoms of my love for you
> Have burst. The tree is full of buds still green
> Myriads. Glistening with the silver sheen
> Of wet warm tears, their quiet pulses new
> With eager life. Like mountain's stream that grew
> From trickling, tiny, ribboned paths between
> Mossed rocks, smooth stones, to thunderous torrent scene,
> And boisterous sparkling waterfall, and blue
> Of lakes, and white of stinging ocean spray.
> Myriads. Like stars in numbers so profound
> I cannot see each light, the Milky Way.
> One blossom on the living tree, one sound
> In nature's symphony. E'en so, I pray,
> My shadow melt with thine to leave the smallest crowned.

Mary Jean also engaged in professional relationships. Statements from her short term in Nepal illustrate. A physician from New Guinea who observed her in Nepal noted: "She was part of a staff quartet . . . a humorous production which revealed Mary Jean as a light-hearted person. It left with me the impression of a person in love with life—a person who knew well the meaning of 'a merry heart doeth good like a medicine,' and one too wise to neglect a vacation and the light side of life."

A doctor at a Nepali leprosy hospital said: "She knew much more medicine than other medical students of her own age and attainments, and I was astonished at her intelligent questions . . . The thirst to acquire knowledge was very great in her."

Clearly, *cultural influences* shaped Mary Jean's story. Boarding school during her elementary years at Woodstock School in the foothills of the Himalayan mountains was one. Another surfaced through diverse truth about science, faith, and humanitarian issues, found in both western and Asian cultures. Through separation from her family during childhood and during her medical study in the United States while her parents worked in Asia, she developed patterns of independence. In her internal debate about the pros and cons of marriage, she processed further dimensions of culture. Interplay between two worlds enhanced the result.

When a Fifth Standard student, Mary Jean's favorite scripture was Proverbs 15. She read from this array of proverbs—many of which deal with wisdom or knowledge—every time she led in morning devotions, once every six weeks. And she recommended it to her classmates who could not decide what to choose for their turn. Family, Mennonite heritage, and religious prominence in India all prompted her to make sense of text through experience. Mary Jean likely valued bits like:

> The eyes of Yahweh are everywhere:
>> observing the evil and the good.

> Glad heart means happy face,
>> where the heart is sad the spirit is broken.

> The way of the lazy is strewn with thorns,
>> the path of the industrious is a broad highway.

Further journal entries show Mary Jean pondering questions of ethics. "We got into an interesting discussion in Science and Human Responsibility class . . . [about] Albert Schweitzer . . . though he meets human need, he is only creating a problem of greater population density . . . similarly, the medical researchist who saves lives only to increase the population problem."

Also, "Shall I tell a starving child I cannot feed him because I feel morally obligated to let him die so that his brothers and sisters can have more food? . . . Can't I at the same time be working with birth control education? . . . Do I have a right to teach methods of birth control to those who 'should' practice it because of their inability to support economically as many children as they would naturally have?"

Further, ". . . the sick came to Jesus who made himself available to them. Do I go out to deal with immediate needs, or should I wait for these to come to my doorstep?"

On the other hand, what might another's "coming to my doorstep" entail? While in medical school, she wrote to her parents: "Last night we had a bit of an incident here at the house which made me think, 'He watching over Israel slumbers not nor sleeps.' . . . I debated a long time whether to write this . . . About 11:00 (p.m.) I thought I heard a door tried . . . Five minutes later another door was tried and someone came into the house. I asked who it was—no answer—then I saw his face emerge around the corner. Unfortunately no hall lights were on. I asked what he wanted. 'Money,' he said. I said I didn't think we could help him very much and began scolding him . . . Asked him what I should do with him—wake up the others (didn't let him know it was all women) or call the police or what . . . We are going to buy some bolts for a few of our windows."

In addition to writing to her parents and sister in India, Mary Jean reflected on word from them: "When they got back, the trunks had arrived. I guess Mother started unpacking . . . Too much reminded her of home and America. God bless my mother. Maybe that's where I get my tendency to dwell on memories. I guess Dad is quite sentimental though, too."

Another matter recurred: "Then, as is expected, the question of marriage comes up . . . I am beginning to realize that I must look at this realistically now or I may fall into something without quite realizing what I'm getting into." Cultural influences rarely hibernate.

Nor did Mary Jean allow matters of faith to be dormant. Values, metaphors, and belief shaped her story. She could not be passive. Neither rigidly autonomous nor self-denigrating, she grew in relationship with God along with others and the world. Through her journal, she expressed budding *theological* convictions.

"Where is the prophet, the bold voice against our complacencies? Or what revolution will it take to make us see the challenge? . . . We tolerate our society's perversions because we have not seen them as evils."

"I have quite strongly come to believe that we cannot tell another person what sin is—all we can do is help a person see Jesus Christ and God."

"Today was my first study of a church. I decided this year I would go to several churches to try to discover what is a meaningful worship experience for me . . . I would say the preacher is not a profound speaker . . . Some may have the oratory and say nothing; I prefer something to be said."

"Whether we are in an area that believes similarly or not, we have a message, through no choice of our own. No matter where I am, I am communicating . . . about what I think is worthwhile . . ." Again, her poetic self gave voice, this time to God her Lover:

> . . .
> You are my lover;
> I am Thy lover.
> Together we love the world
> And little ones.
> We love the flower faces even when all petals have fallen
> We love the star patterns, and the rain sounds.
> We love the feeling of the neighbor's furry kitten
>   and stroke her with a tenderness.
>   But she prefers the sun to Thee and me.
> What do You and I prefer?
> We love the world and love each other;
> Thee and me are lovers.

"I believe I will start recording the Gospel passages where Jesus told someone to do something and see what pattern we can expose."

During the final month of her life, Mary Jean studied the book of Isaiah and printed two pages side-by-side in her notebook—one with the person's words/response to God, the other with the words of God.

Pastor John Mosemann said at her memorial service: "She knew ultimate truth was found in the way of faith."

What *virtues* have yet to be named? Not a passive person for whom miracles occur, Mary Jean was witty, talented, disciplined, and adventuresome. Further, she was ambitious, in that she exercised courage and knew personal power. Herself wise, she practiced Wisdom. Part of that meant to take risks.

A grade school classmate at Woodstock in India remembers: "On long forays to the stream thousands of feet down the valley, she always collected more ferns than anyone. Once just the two of us and my big dog went down, and got thoroughly lost. It was real adventure. Home again, we had dozens of ferns—some fairly rare ones—and 27 leeches between us!"

Sixth Standard roommate Marj remembers: "We used to play one of the old crank-up type record players at night by putting it under the bedclothes and replacing the regular needle with a sewing needle! Granted, we couldn't hear much of the music. Our next door neighbor would knock on the wall if she heard anything—to keep us from getting caught by the ever-roving teacher on duty!"

During school vacations, Mary Jean and her older sister Joann memorized poetry for fun. Later, her friends often asked her at slumber parties to recite "The Congo." With great gusto she boomed, "boomlay, boomlay, boomlay, boom." She also loved to tell gruesome stories and was a master of the muffled scream.

When beginning college, she wrote: "God, help me to trust You more, to love You and others better, and to be humble. Those three things just now are some of the most important things to me."

Mary Jean developed an organized way of doing things, whether studying for a test, writing a term paper, cleaning her room, or deciding what she believed. For example: "I made a new resolve to tithe my time and put two hours [per day] into devotions. God help me . . . I don't want to make this period only an 'ought.'" Later, she pursued a further discipline: "I want to try more of an ascetic life . . . Cut down eating to show that the body need not get an upper hand . . . My attempt has not been successful and I wonder whether my reliance is on self rather than God."

But Mary Jean's dependence seems crystal clear. Her coin purse always contained a tiny note, meant only to remind herself: "Not too poor to share." On her desk stood a card with her favorite prayer of St. Francis of Assisi. Will and Wisdom merged: "It seems that so much of the studying here asks for good discernment—to judge what is the most valuable rather than to try to learn everything."

Ever reflective and thoughtful, in fact profoundly so, Mary Jean left more self-revealing gems. *Feelings and attitudes* tumble from her journal. Living in Goshen when a young teen, she observed: "Eighth Street is strange and lonely in the early morning. The rising sun forces tree patterns on the pavement and sidewalk . . . Even our lawn tingles with the sun. Silver dew reflections blind out the green . . . Only the continuous hum of the factory, the regular streams of gray and black smoke, indicate the night did not mean newness and refreshment for many."

Self-critical, but not destructively so, she wrote: "I believe one of the greatest weapons against God in my life, and one of my worst enemies, is discouragement... My apology for asking you to be sorry for me ... I am able to see through my wrong attitude."

We always perceive Truth in distinct ways after a person's death. A statement and two accounts of Mary Jean's prompt me to pause in holy awe: "Endings are always stranger and lonelier than beginnings because they hold experience behind them."

"I'm so glad for Christmas vacation! ... Dad took care of Adlai Stevenson's son today, as an emergency case. He was in a wreck near Middlebury (Indiana). Four boys were going home from Harvard; two were killed. God, comfort those families! I think it would be awful to have someone suddenly die for whom you had planned and dreamed a future and all . . ."

Two years before Mary Jean's death, the wombat and bandicoot were mentioned in a medical class. She learned that the rat-like bandicoot can bother the grain farmers in south India and Ceylon or can be a marsupial in Tasmania and New Guinea. With interest whetted, she wrote to her sister Ruth in India:

> E'en the wombat and the bandicoot
> Were synthesized.
> Perhaps within Thy mind, perhaps without.
> At any rate, by Thee.
> > Strength of flesh divided by weakness of the mind
> > Permits survival with struggle.
> > This may be smooth and constant, expectedly rhythmic,
> > Or syncopated.
> > Later, there is death.
> But I cannot say the wombat is a "slouch."
> Nor can I say the bandicoot's a "sluggard."
> These do not die because they never tried;
> These die because they were synthesized.
> Why die I?

Afterword—Whereas some exceptional women intimidate others less gifted, Mary Jean Yoder inspires. Her story serves as incentive for life. Having read a portion of it here, you will choose what to retell or what to imitate.

During her final trip to India, Mary Jean had purchased the craft piece pictured with this article. When I returned from there in 1965, her mother gave it to me. From my study wall, it reminds me of friendship. Its procession leads me on, beyond the memory of "I cannot live without my macaroon."

19

My Rebirthing to Womanhood

Mattie Marie Mast[*]

Anticipate the story's subject to speak with new authority.
She highlights mutuality that neither denies self nor glorifies
autonomy. She interprets personal thought and meaning,
addressing stereotypes created by church and family.

Dear Daughter,

When you were only eight years old, you asked me a question which was to change me later, at midlife. One day as you were playing, you came running into the house to abruptly ask, "Mommy, could God have a daughter like he had a son Jesus?" I remember I stared at you in disbelief. I did not know what to say. I groped for syllables that would make sense. Exasperated and impotent, I sent you to Dad. I followed not far behind and overheard your theologian Dad clear his throat a few times before he lamely said, "I guess he could have."

If you had been older, I would have wondered what you were reading to trigger such a question. But since you were only eight, I received the inquiry as an inquisitive thought. The question was legitimate and genuine. It lodged like a seed deep within me. This is the

---

[*]Mattie Marie Mast served twenty-five years in northern Argentina with Mennonite Board of Missions. Leaving that work gave occasion to process the past. She now writes letters from Pennsylvania.

story of how it took root, burst open, gave birth, and continues to grow. You are eighteen years old now, and I want you to be the first to hear my story.

The Mystery of Birth—Mystery accompanies any birth. Life is proof that birthing took place. But that cannot diminish the awe experienced during the initial life-giving. I have known similar wonder through my birthing into fuller womanhood. New life rushed through me. How could I feel so differently and still be the same woman? Why did it happen to me?

Life took on new dimensions. What changed radically were the perspectives with which I saw my world, the words I read, and the people I met. It was like beginning to live anew. It was as if up to this point, only a fraction of me had been alive.

Before this rebirth experience, I never thought of myself as a dominated woman. Your Dad and I were a typical, happy, Christian couple. We had our conflicts, as do all couples. But we talked, and we respected each others' opinions. I never felt a need to be "liberated," as some did. I never sought it. I was quite content with my life.

So how and why did this happen to me? I avidly sought God's will for my life, to understand what following Christ means. My rebirthing into womanhood has been an integral part of spiritual renewal and living the fullness of the Good News of Christ. It does not have to do with being capricious but with understanding the Good News in more of its entirety.

Our God is a God of full-life for all women and men, for all ethnic groups. Our Creator does not offer lameness or second class status, but dignity and integrity of being. As daughters and sons of God, we are expected to be all that God's image can reflect, within each of us. Otherwise, we mock our Creator. Christians can never accept as God's will the domination of one person over another, or of one ethnic group over another.

Ask your Dad someday to tell his side of the rebirthing. He walked alongside me and together each of us was reborn in our own way.

The Impregnations—In retrospect, I see various impregnations that led to my rebirthing as a woman. Your question disquieted me. It suggested the need to use female images when speaking about God, rather than refer to God as if only or primarily male. It suggested that we are born with a need for wholeness. I remember jotting down your question, to record its cuteness in your baby book. But as time went by, your question became much deeper than a cute remark. It set into motion within me new discoveries of God, a new sense of my relation to the Creator.

For more than fifteen years our family had been walking in solidarity with the Argentine Toba Church and community. With the Tobas, I had become acutely aware of the evil forces of discrimination, marginalization, and domination. These anti-life forces stood in direct conflict with the biblical message of wholeness. I realize now that this had profoundly sensitized me. Seeds were being sown and impregnation was taking place for my own rebirthing.

Other impregnations occurred, as my spiritual pilgrimage included Catholic charismatic renewal. In a setting where deep suspicions between Evangelical and Catholic groups remain, for me to receive spiritual blessing from Catholics was Providential. It opened my eyes to God's sovereignty and my finiteness. It predisposed me to radical changes in all areas of my life.

The gestation period lasted nine to ten years. Catholic spiritual support groups were like an embracing womb, holding securely the impregnations experienced until they could develop into full gestation. Catholic Christians provided warmth, nurture, and protection from exposure. We loved each other through differences. We worshipped, as kindred beings, the same God, Jesus the Christ, and the Holy Spirit. Within this *agape* I felt free to confess sins and to open my life to transforming Power. The embryo grew.

I am Reborn a Woman—The real impetus, or final push of labor, that rebirthed me into fuller womanhood was seeing Mary, the mother of Jesus, revealed in her humanness. Mary as woman. God chose her to be the mother of Jesus because she was woman. In this way, God affirmed all women. God could surely have birthed Jesus in some other way, bypassing woman as had been man.

Catholics emphasize Mary's qualities in ways that Evangelicals stress Paul's or Peter's. Simply to hear her womanhood frequently affirmed made me feel special, because I am also woman. As she had a unique role, as woman, in God's plan toward salvation, so I am called of God to particular tasks because I am woman. What she performed, man could not do.

Rebirth Accompanied by Joy and Pain—Both joy and pain accompany birth. The joy I felt with my rebirth to womanhood was not a giddy mirth. It was intense, a convulsing joy that sent tremors through me. I was the same person, yet new and restored.

For the first time in my life, I felt a bonding with other women. I wanted to share this Good News of fuller womanhood with other women, especially Christian women. I began to look for articles and books that focused on and gave worth to women's particular agenda. I reread portions of the Bible. I was like a starved person searching for food.

My rebirthing had to do with wholeness, with shalom, with justice and full humanity. It had to do with being faithful to the Good News of Jesus' inclusion, with proclaiming the whole Gospel, not a partial dimension. It had to do with owning my gift of sexuality as expressed in Genesis 1:27—in the image of God male *and* female were created. It had to do with authentic mutuality rather than woman or man's distinct power. Therefore, full participation, not chain-of-command or hierarchy, became an authentic mode. My rebirthing had to do with being of the same value in God's eyes, judged worthy whether female or male. New birth meant to live out that truth.

There was pain too. My eyes had been opened as a woman. What I saw and experienced was overwhelming. There was discrimination against women in the newspapers, at the corner store, during church services, even in our own home. I experienced anger. I grieved. I grieved because I felt betrayed by my good religious roots. Your Dad and I both grieved.

As a church we have been operating like a person with only one lung. But two lungs contribute to a full, healthy life. Instead of wholeness, we have been content with the partial, with being maimed. What correlation is there between almost exclusive male imagery for God and "keeping women in their place" in our churches and communities? I realized that our religious expression has mirrored our cultural prejudices rather than being prophetic, biblical, and life-giving.

I lived through profound changes. At times I was perplexed. I realized that I would never again be the same. This was painful and frustrating and at the same time empowering. How can I channel this pain and anger into constructive being and doing, I wondered. How can I accommodate both the biblical ideal and the reality we live?

The Tobas are my Model—I went to the Tobas for help. As I sat with them, I observed and learned from them. I found that my rebirthing to womanhood resembled their rebirth experience of salvation and Indianness. Yet, their being marginalized within society had been more destructive, overall. How do they cope, I wondered again.

The Tobas are re-affirmed in their identity as Indians when they accept Jesus the Christ. Their faith claims their being created in the image of God. To acknowledge their Indian identity further empowers them. Knowing God loves their being Indian causes them to take legitimate pride in themselves. The Gospel offers full-life

for the Indians here in this world and in the world to come. Full-life for Tobas means living life with dignity, being respected for their cultural qualities, and claiming the right to be themselves.

I also learned from Toba example that as Christians they own their Indian identity in order to serve others. Through service to others, Tobas share their soulful Gospel with most of the neighboring tribes. Pride in their Indian identity helps them to better serve in God's Way.

I observed that not all Tobas constructively handle the anger prompted by the cruel reality of domination and prejudice. Some of them lash out when they are frustrated. Others demand immediate or abrupt changes. When their prophetic voices are ignored, some become casualties to the cause of justice and full-life. However, wise Toba leaders advise their people how to function in the dominant system. At the same time they counsel never to compromise their goal of full-life. The Good News of full-life for all can never be negotiated.

Conclusion—Further elements related to my rebirthing will likely surface; I hope to perceive them as they emerge. Radical changes are never simplistic. I have learned, however, that the gift of fullness comes through channels, events, and people often not credited by socialized human criteria. Great wisdom often resides in a child, an oppressed minority, or a marginalized religious group.

On the other hand, when I attend to Jesus' teaching and life, I see how my experience connects with his thought and action. His young mother Mary originated from Galilee, that part of Palestine thought to be full of second-class Jews. Precisely from that area came the mother of the Christ. Unexpectedly, the greatest gift in human history came through a woman from Galilee.

My daughter, that is part of my story. It is not finished. In many ways I feel that it is only beginning. Thanks again for your question. Keep asking them!

Love,

Your mother

20

Letters From China

*Lynda Nyce and Gretchen Nyce**

> *Anticipate that these adventurous reporters will be conscious about their feelings linked to experiences. To extend credit to women writers is to let them express what is central for them.*

[Editor's Note: People at Goshen College (Indiana) value international experience. Many faculty members have lived in countries other than North America for several years. A good number of international students share out of their distinct cultures. A Study Service Term (SST) in another country has been expected of Goshen College students for twenty-five years. The twelfth year of a student exchange with China occurred in 1992; this exchange will be renewed in 1996.

Each group of twenty GC students experiences China through friendships at Sichuan Teacher's University, Chengdu. They live on-campus. In addition to language study, lectures about history, culture, and literature, field trips to important events and places, and individual

---

*Lynda Nyce is completing her Sociology PhD. dissertation at the University of Notre Dame, Indiana, with a focus on homelessness. Other cross-cultural encounters included a half year in India and a summer of Voluntary Service with Hispanic children in San Antonio, Texas. Gretchen Nyce also valued a semester of high school at Kodaikanal International School in southern India. She now teaches math at Wawasee High School and is an assistant coach at Goshen College.

contacts, Goshen students teach conversational English to Chinese students in the first two years of university.

Our daughters had this unique opportunity when juniors in college, Lynda in 1989 and Gretchen in 1991. Both were good letter writers (though when writing, neither knew the letters would later appear in print). These excerpts reflect on cultural features or insight into women's experience.

Excerpts of letters from Lynda:

Dear Mom & Dad,

22 August, 1989—Greetings from a train in China, somewhere towards Xian. We have been on the train for 18 1/2 hours so far . . .

My first impression of China from the airplane was that this really was a different country . . . in the Beijing airport, the communist difference became evident, with soldiers on guard and a very plain, uncommercial airport . . .

As we drove through Beijing, I kept being reminded of scenes in India. Despite China's enormous population, the streets seemed so empty compared to New Delhi . . .

We went straight from the airport to Tiananmen Square. I couldn't believe they were taking us there first. Maybe an attempt to show us that everything was fine and 'back to normal' . . .

In the afternoon, we went to the Great Wall. There was a certain specialness about seeing that wonder in the rain and mist . . .

[At the train station] . . . I spent about 20 minutes . . . with three men who were trying to ask me questions . . . It was very frustrating to not be able to communicate quickly, but I learned a lot and felt I made some progress . . .

5 Sept. 1989—On Thursday we went to town . . . we explored back streets. I found some good bargains on a tea cup, bowl, and some paintings. The art vendors set up very beautiful displays just outside the shops and Jin Jiang hotel. We went down a street lined with tailors set up under canopies. All the small specialty shops crack me up—nuts and bolts, tires, plastic baskets and bowls, small engine parts, electrical wire, telephones and wiring, etc. shops . . .

Getting used to dancing face-to-face (actually I'm a head taller) with a Chinese woman took a bit of time . . . Chinese have a totally different view of personal space—they seem to not need nearly as much as we . . .

At 7:30 Mr. Xu came over and translated the official government movie about May-June [Tiananmen] activities . . . quite interesting, to say the least . . .

[W]ent running. Running at night through the nearby streets is great! I feel very safe around here and do not get paranoid about people staring at me—that's just part of life. But at night, you don't get stared at because by the time they figure out that we look different, we're past them . . .

[W]e walked to a silk embroidery factory. Workers were embroidering very beautiful wall hangings and screens—very expensive items. We asked our interpreter why there were so many female workers and a couple men. He said that "though there are many women, the men are the masters" . . . Overall, I have been excited to see the equality on jobs—the female bus drivers, professors, and factory workers are apparently equal to men . . .

I walked out the back gate and out the path into the country. People are harvesting rice and working in the fields. I was pretty much in my own world and singing to feel better. I finally noticed that an older woman was standing beside the path, talking to me and pointing to her house. She was pleasant looking and smiled sincerely, so I went in. She brought me a big tin cup full of tea and something that was breaded and fried. I think it might have been pork. Her husband also came. Gradually, the crowd grew to six around me. We tried to communicate, succeeded a bit, smiled a lot . . . I felt a bit foolish and embarrassed, but soaked up the kindness, openness and cultural experience . . .

13 Sept. 1989—. . . We were just as interested in their method of construction as in the park itself. We took pictures of the workers (equal distribution of men and women) . . . Ms. Shang went with us and taught us Chinese phrases along the way. She's a neat person to talk to . . . Her English is very limited, so I am forced to learn more Chinese, but she's very patient . . .

After Wu Ho, we went to the Children's Palace, a place where children go for violin, painting, calligraphy, and dance lessons . . . over 60 children were playing violin at the same time—some as young as 4, the oldest about 12. The little ones were playing the 1st movement of Mozart's "Eine Kleine Nacht Musik," something some high school kids in the States have trouble with . . . They expected me to play violin with an 11 year old girl who had placed 2nd in her age group in a national competition . . . I was really excited to sit among children and communicate through the language of music . . . then we listened to a 6-year-old play a Beethoven piece. Incredible! . . .

20 Sept., 1989—. . . Monday Richard and I taught our first class of sophomores. That was great fun! They were eager to see us and seem like they want to learn . . . I tried to teach them a song. We read it, sang it, and weren't getting too far when one student said "Maybe it was too hard." (Favorite words used by students have been "maybe, perhaps, and I think.") Remembering that church singing three weeks ago, I began writing the do, re, mi, etc. syllables above the words. They <u>immediately</u> could sing the song. I was thrilled! . . .

27 Sept. 1989—. . . The wonderfully sinful bakery is near there. On the other side of the road are faculty family apartment buildings. Everyone who works or studies here lives here. The campus is quite large . . .

After lunch I biked into town to meet Winnie. Winnie is the daughter of a doctor here in Chengdu and she wants an English-speaking friend . . . She's a neat person and I really enjoyed myself . . .

At times I feel like an English-speaking robot. People always say, "I'm glad to meet you so that I can practice my English." Seemingly, they want an English tool without opinions rather than sincere friendship . . .

4 Oct. 1989—. . . In the Buddhist monasteries, I was struck again with the idea that God exists for all. We have different ways of connecting with God. I could feel worshipful and prayerful in those monasteries . . . I offered one of my candles to a Buddha form but didn't do the three bows, and I know God understood that gesture as being an identification with culture, not a sacrilegious thing. The monks watching me were greatly pleased . . .

11 Oct. 1989—. . . After Chinese class, we began our Taiji Quan classes— ancient Chinese shadow boxing. Taiji is an exercise that many older people do to help them with physical ailments and concentration. The idea behind Taiji is for the person to clear her/his mind and think of nothing but the movements the body is making. Body movements begin in the mind . . .

18 Oct. 1989—. . . Then we asked the class about jobs in China. They cannot get any summer work unless their parents own a business or they tutor children. My students are studying to be teachers of English. Upon graduation, they will be assigned a school in some area of China, and there they must remain . . .

Held at the new Sichuan Jiang Arts Center downtown, the music and dance extravaganza was really incredible. A professional group of dancers from Shanghai performed for two hours. The building was the first impressive thing . . . The show was a conglomeration of dances/music from the Tang, Song, and Ming dynasties as well as modern stuff. At times the changes between periods or styles was abrupt, almost humorous. The most incredible parts were the elaborate costumes and quick costume changes. Beautiful silks, brocades, muslins, elaborate masks, and beautiful sets . . . Even the audience was different in decorum . . .

. . . We headed to a girls' dorm. Amazing how over 100 people can watch one TV, which is inside a 1st floor dorm window, facing outside . . .

24 Oct. 1989—We left Chengdu Friday at 4:00 p.m. and traveled 23 1/2 hours to Kunming. The train trip was excellent . . . The scenery was incredibly beautiful. The train left Chengdu and the plains, climbing upwards through tunnels, over rivers, between mountains, terraced fields, and past time-untouched-villages to the 1,820 mile-above-sea-level plateau where Kunming is . . . the green of the rice fields and trees, the red soil, peasants working in fields and rice paddies, mud brick houses, and gushing rivers. Amazing!

. . . then we boarded the bus to go downtown to the beginning spots for the races . . . I was dropped off at the 10k starting area . . . 8,400 people ran in the three events—5,000 in the 5k, 3,000 in the 10k, and 400 in the marathan . . .

. . . All the foreigners were given special seats in the stands and we all met the mayor and vice mayor of Kunming . . . I still can't believe I ran in a 10k in China (sponsored by the International Olympic Committee), at 6,000 feet altitude, in a strange city, with cameras following me everywhere . . .

People in Kunming really do look different from the Han people of Beijing, Xian, and Chengdu . . .

8 Nov. 1989—. . . *we had a lecture on Confucianism. That was superb! It was given by Professor Luo, a female prof from Sichuan University in town . . . She's simply an amazing woman. A prof of Shakespeare and other classical writers, her English is practically flawless. She is incredibly intelligent, and expresses herself like no other Chinese woman I have met . . . she translated some Confucian writings and added her commentary. She expressed disagreement and criticism of points in his work, giving her position. So refreshing . . .*

14 Nov. 1989—. . . *I'm trying to explore issues of family life in China by interviewing a few people from various backgrounds . . . I'm about to the point of explosion because I want to share all of what I've heard and been amazed by . . .*

. . . when the subject turns to male/female relations, they can be very archaic . . . I'm always amazed that in this country which has equality of pay, positions, etc. in urban areas for men and women, there still exists such a distinction between male and female roles . . .

21 Nov. 1989—. . . *At 2:00 Dr. Enmei [see H. Burkholder's article about her], an 86 year old medical doctor, came to talk with us. She is an amazing woman. She spent from 1951 to 1978 in Communist prisons and camp. For 19 months during the Cultural Revolution she was in solitary confinement. Truly incredible that she survived such an experience. We talked with her for two hours. After all those years of wasted time, she holds no resentment towards the Communists and now works for the Department of Public Health . . .*

2 Dec. 1989—. . . *Friday's performance went better than I had expected . . . Really amazing that here we sit in the middle of a communist country and feel okay about reenacting the Christian Christmas story . . .*

. . . a few of us went to Mr. She's house for dinner. He is the man who I read for a couple weeks ago and he has done a lot of translating for us . . . We had a great meal. His wife and mother prepared all the food but did not join us. That made me really *uncomfortable. It's an act of their cultural upbringing that I could never get used to . . .*

. . . a little anxious about coming back, not sure why exactly. Just that as I've said before, reality is here and at home perhaps nothing will have changed. But things have changed and there's no doubt I have as well . . .

The cooks invited us into the kitchen to make baozi for dinner. That was great, yet I never succeeded in getting good-looking baozi made . . .

Take care of yourselves. I'll talk with you soon! I miss you both.

Love, Lynda

Excerpts of letters from Gretchen:

Mom and Dad,

Aug. 24, 1991—Yesterday [in Beijing] we went to the Ming Tombs . . . a bunch of underground chambers with thrones and tombs for some emperors and empresses.

Then we went to the Great Wall. It was awesome! We totally wore ourselves out by jogging up part of it . . . On the way down my legs were shaking from the exercise . . .

After supper a bunch of us (six guys and I) went to the basketball courts on the campus where we are staying, to see if we could play. Some Chinese guys were shooting so we walked onto the court and when the ball came to us, we started shooting with them. They knew no English, so J.J. counted to five in Chinese, pointed at them and pointed at us. They nodded but only four wanted to play. So they pointed at our tallest guy, for him to be on their team. We said o.k. Everybody going by stopped to watch, so we had a large crowd all around the court. It was a lot of fun.

Sept. 3, 1991—Today we went into town [Chengdu] for the second time. We figured out the bus system the first time in town and it's quite easy (and cheap).

I've met a few Chinese students so far and a young professor. He is a linguistics prof and said he would like to teach me about the ancient Chinese writing and I could help him improve his English. The Chinese are always so eager to be instant friends—which is foreign to me, but I'll try to be accommodating . . .

I also met this old, somewhat mentally handicapped man one afternoon when I was shooting baskets. I let him shoot with me which made him very happy. I don't think anybody pays attention to him. He always comes and watches us play in the evenings and says "Ni hao" ("Hi") to me

. . .

We are keeping in touch with the situation in the Soviet Union (or should I say disUnion) through short wave and USA Today (about a week late). There are also five Azerbaijani students here who also give us details.

Sept. 20, 1991—. . . First, I'll answer a few of your questions. A "friendship store" is a huge store with everything under the sun (or at least under the sun in China).

. . . We just returned from a concert of traditional Chinese music. It was really interesting. We were all amazed at the sounds they could get out of those instruments . . .

One of the best things about living in a Communist University is that everyone connected with the University lives on campus. There are old, retired people and children of workers and faculty. It adds a diversity that you can't get at a college at home . . .

I've made many connections with Chinese people during the last few weeks . . . I went to a park with a very interesting couple. They both speak English well and have good jobs where they get to do international traveling. They treated me to lunch (I have no idea what we ate!) . . .

Then last weekend, Mr. Gong (head of the English department) took me into town to meet friends of his. It's a family of doctors—the father works at a hospital, the mother teaches at a medical college, and their daughter (who's 23) works at a hospital for a huge factory . . . On Thursday I went back there and went to the zoo with Jiang Ning (the daughter). It's nice to have these off-campus connections. I'm sure I'll see these people often.

So far I've enjoyed trying to answer everyone's questions at English Corner (a regular time to meet informally to practice speaking English). They have quite a broad range of questions, and it's quite a challenge to give them all good answers. Li Bo (the noisy little boy) came and found me there last time. So, I held him and put him on my shoulders while talking to people. He chatters . . .

October 2, 1991—Hello again! . . . on to the field trip. We were gone for three days. This was a holiday weekend; October 1st marks the beginning of the People's Republic. We went to Mt. Emei and the Giant Buddha. I really enjoyed the places . . .

The second day we climbed Mt. Emei . . . Three guys and I took off up the mountain to see the wild monkeys. After about an hour, it started to get really steep (the whole path was laid with concrete or stone steps). One section had a couple hundred steps straight up which felt like we were on an escalator! We got in a rhythm and couldn't feel ourselves picking our legs up 'cause they were numb from the exertion. If we looked down, the steps appeared to be receding below us; it was so weird! . . . we decided to go back down and count every stairstep. We half jogged down so it wouldn't hurt our legs so much . . . There were 4,704 steps one way . . . Later we looked at a map and realized that we had climbed up over 1,000 meters in elevation. And we did it in 1 1/2 hours! If that's not hiking, then I don't know what is . . .

October 16, 1991—. . . I started teaching about the time I wrote my last letter. It's going pretty well. I have 26 freshmen (15 females and 11 males) They come from wealthy city families and peasant families, so it's quite a mix. Many females and peasants are rather shy, but they're improving. The first day I introduced myself and showed them pictures I'd brought, gave them English names, and had them introduce themselves. They would stand up whenever they spoke! If they asked a question, they'd remain standing until I'd answered it, and said 'Thank you.' I had to explain to them that this is an informal class and that they did not need to stand . . .

October 29, 1991—. . . We've had a few really awesome days lately . . . a few of us went out and threw my aerobie around. I don't think the Chinese had ever seen one before, so as usual we were the day's entertainment. Li Bo came out and managed to get it stuck in a tree . . .

Today is Tuesday, our day to go downtown . . . I had one of my wildest bus rides on the way back. The female bus driver drove like a maniac. We passed within an inch of many big trucks and buses and came close to running over numerous bicyclists. The market area was very crowded, but she just went blasting through with the horn blaring (honking for 2/3 of the 25-minute trip). She was wearing a jean jacket which said "Cheerful" on the back! (The Chinese like to put English words on clothing, whether or not it makes sense.)

November 7-10, 1991—. . . The last few days I've had some really good experiences with my students. They are really opening up and enjoying class . . . Last night I went to the room of a sophomore . . . She's a lot of fun and we had a good time talking and playing cards. That is, until 10:30, the usual time for lights to be shut off . . .

Last night I went for a cooking lesson. Shang Kai invited us over in groups of 4-5 to learn to cook. She is very energetic and speaks English well. She and her husband taught us how to make many dishes; they're all very simple. We had to go to the market during the day, to buy vegetables and pork—on our own. She told us that we had picked a good piece of meat . . .

November 28, 1991—Today we had a big Thanksgiving dinner for lunch. We did most of the cooking and work ourselves and invited all the Waiban [foreigners' assistance department of the university] staff to come (60 people) . . .

On Sunday I went to Jiang Ning's house and had a wonderful time with her family. We went to the market to get supplies for making Jiaozi [pork-filled dumplings] and then made and ate them. We had a big "Chinglish" conversation.

Jeff and I have been learning the abacus from a professor's daughter here. On Saturday we will go to their house for supper and our last lesson . . .

An international women's soccer tournament is being held in China, so I've been able to watch some games on TV . . .

I'm getting excited about Goshen College basketball and Christmas. I can't wait to give all my gifts! . . . Take care and I'll see you in Chicago!

Love, Gretchen

21

More Than Hints of Heritage

Pat Hostetter Martin[*]

Anticipate creative writing plus details and feelings, some that others might overlook. Effective writers reveal oft-hidden realities. They interpret personal meaning or identify what is valued and why. Specific social and historical setting matters, as does truthfulness.

Pat Hostetter grew up in Harrisonburg, Virginia, in a preacher's family with eight rambunctious children. Holidays were spent with a large extended family of aunts, uncles and cousins at the 200-year-old stone farmhouse of maternal grandparents Milton and Ruth Brackbill in Frazer, Pennsylvania.

On the farm the old carriage house, the spring house, and the chicken house were renovated into cottages that were rented out, along with some of the bedrooms in the fifteen-room farmhouse. Pat and her sister and cousins spent many a summer hanging up sheets and towels, making beds, cleaning cottages, and marveling at the variety of people who discovered the old-fashioned hospitality of the Brackbill's Motel.

After college, Pat joined the Mennonite Central Committee in 1964 to work in Vietnam. During her three years there, she met and

---

married Earl Martin. Together with two small children, they returned to Vietnam in 1973 and stayed until the end of the war in 1975.

Later their family lived in the large, southern Philippine island of Mindanao for three-and-a-half years, where they worked with a Catholic Social Action Center. They then served as Co-Secretaries for MCC's East Asia programs.

Pat reflects on her journey. She agrees with David Hare that "the act of writing is the act of discovering what you believe." She believes that the journey of discovering and living out one's unique womanly gifts is a journey to be taken alone. It involves a "revolution from within" as Gloria Steinem suggests. And Pat claims imagination as one of the first steps on the journey of self-discovery. "If we cannot imagine, if we do not dream, we will not create."

While she is two generations beyond, Pat often finds inspiration in the memories of her grandmother, as she tries to balance a demanding job with family life and other creative pursuits.

Letter read at my 94-year-old Grandmother Brackbill's grave

November 20, 1989

Dear Grandma,

When I heard on Thursday that you were "going home," I felt a surge of joy. You would be closer to us again, I thought. Your place in Sarasota never seemed like your home to me. I kept seeing you in a larger space—a place with giant oaks, a meandering creek, and mint-filled meadow. I saw you bending at wash tubs of steaming, white sheets; presiding over long tables mounded with food from the "little Mennonite garden"; and greeting guests, from all walks of life, with warmth and hospitality.

Your grandson, Minh, likes to talk about "making memories." Well, none of us were quite aware at the time of just how many memories were in the making over the years. But I had a sense of <u>deja vu</u> journeying here to commemorate your homecoming. Little bursts of "Over the river and through the woods to Grandmother's house we go" kept singing in my head. Today there were only three children in the car instead of eight, but the excitement of seeing Grandpa and aunts and uncles and cousins was keen. And you, Grandma, as usual, are at the center of our celebration.

You and I, Grandma, are a part of a stream that keeps flowing—not unlike the creek that continues to run through Beulah's Park—even though history and people change around us. My memory spans five generations of women in this clan, from Grandma Haldeman to my daughter, Lara. It's a lineage of strong women—gentle yet determined—not unlike water. Lao Tse, a Chinese sage, once said, "Under heaven nothing is more soft and yielding than water. Yet for attacking the solid and strong, nothing is better."

Your current in this stream of history has reached the ocean this week, Grandma, and now you can rest, absorbed by the Great Almighty who offered, "come unto me all you who labor and are heavy laden and I will give you rest." But the memories flow on and there are a million of them.

Friday, as I rubbed Ben Gay into Lara's sore arm muscle, I could see your brown, plaid medicine case and smell the pungent odors. Last night I found myself washing up the odds and ends of dishes on our sink, something I don't normally do, and I wondered whether your spirit was nudging me to clean up the kitchen before I went to bed.

Today when I saw Judy, I remembered the time when I playfully tried to scare her in the shower and accidentally slit the shower curtain with my comb. To come to you and say, "I'm sorry," was always so hard.

Grandma, there's one last memory before you go. Remember all the little gifts you and Grandpa brought back with you from your trips? Well, those treasures made in exotic places like Japan and China still grace my shelves and chests. I want you to take this small vase along with you as my present for your journey. It's filled with dried flowers from my garden. Let it be one last memory between us.

Grandma, I loved you,
Pat (signed)

Written on a flight to Asia immediately after my Grandmother Brackbill's funeral

Tuesday, 21 November, 1989
A thousand thoughts have gone through my head over the past 24 hours since I tucked a vase of dried flowers into the satin cloth that covered Grandma Brackbill's body.

After the viewing (a funny word, isn't it?), Grandpa, with his children and grandchildren and great grandchildren around him, said together John 14:1-3:

Let not your heart be troubled: ye believe in God, believe also in me. In my Father's house are many mansions: if it were not so, I would have told you. I go to prepare a place for you. And if I go and prepare a place for you, I will come again, and receive you unto myself; that where I am, there ye may be also.

We then sang some of Grandpa's favorite songs, "When the Roll Is Called Up Yonder, I'll Be There," and "Precious Name, Oh, How Sweet." Then Grandpa, ever in charge, announced the time was right to close the casket. Inside lay the frail little body of Grandma, light as a feather—the unbearable lightness of non-being.

The two pictures—one of Grandma and one of Grandpa in their youth—that had been tucked by Grandpa into the satin flounce of the open casket lid were removed. Wherever they had lived, pictures of family had literally covered their walls, cupboards, and bulletin boards.

Grandpa's flair had often brought natural beauty into their home as well. Lush red tomatoes or full, green peppers or bunches of juicy, purple grapes might be brought in from the garden, still attached to their vines. Grandpa would hang them from the lamp above the kitchen table or drape them along a window sill. He was in tune with the art of nature.

Grandma was much more practical. She grew picturesque, miniature gardens of chives, onions, and lettuce in pans or boxes on her back porch—to say nothing of the beautiful and orderly "little Mennonite garden" that she and Max worked at together during earlier years.

But there was a finality today to Grandma's life—something that Grandpa seemed to accept, something he had likely anticipated for a long time. Grandma had become hard to care for; no one could help her quite like Grandpa. He had been patient and loving with her even though he was often tired. And when she died quietly in her sleep, he was content. "Jesus took Mama home," he told Aunt Miriam.

Eight grandchildren representing each of the five daughters' families carried the absurdly large casket slowly out to the cemetery at the Frazer Church. I wish she could have been buried in the old Frazer graveyard where Grandpa and Grandma Haldeman were buried. I think Grandma would have liked to hear and feel the trains rumble by. But the old Frazer Church is long gone and the small, garden-like plot, surrounded by beautiful, old trees, is now tucked between a garish shopping center and the Pennsylvania Railroad.

The new Frazer cemetery seems open and unprotected, without trees or fence, as housing developments encroach. Grandpa Brackbill's older brother, Charlie, is buried there and Grandma is now beside him—something that did not bypass the Brackbill daughters. Ever looking for an amusing story, they had recently found an old letter from Uncle Charlie to the then nubile, Ruth Haldeman, asking her, in flowery language, for a date. But apparently, the youngest Brackbill brother had already caught her fancy. The aunts concluded that Grandma could rest peacefully beside Uncle Charlie but hardly beside Uncle Harry, also buried close by!

The procession to the gravesite proceeded solemnly. Ever conscious of his witness to the community, Grandpa again started singing. The strains, picked up in ragged fashion down the straggling line of family and friends, were quickly wafted away by the stiff breeze.

The afternoon was beautiful—warmer again after several bitterly cold days, overcast and windy. Grandpa led in another song as we stood around the open grave, its starkness muted somewhat by the artificial, green grass laid down by Mauer's Funeral Home. For this family, that was hardly necessary.

I had asked to read a letter I composed to Grandma on Thursday, the day she died. Since I was not going to be able to be at the memorial service in the evening, I wanted to pay my last respects to a woman I had grown to love. The letter was full of memories and hope, and I was able to read it without tears. I don't know why, for afterward I stood and shook, partly from the wind but mostly from emotion.

Catherine Browning, in the Fall 1989 issue of *Creation* magazine, writes about "mysterium tremendum." She says:

> in that unsuspecting hour when we tremble from the
> core of our being, we reclaim our earthiness, our
> humility, our vulnerability as children of the Universe.
> We acknowledge the force trying to catch our attention.
> We experience our bodies in a new way. We respond to

the rest of creation with a heightened sense of awareness. This response, this submission frees us to be responsible stewards of Mother Earth.

Now I realize that this "mysterium tremendum" was precisely what had happened to me as a teenager when drawn into the night, as I often was, to lie under the stars to contemplate the mystery of the universe. I would sometimes become so overwhelmed with fascination, imagination and fear that I would need to go indoors to feel some protection.

Another occasion when I was overwhelmed with "mysterium tremendum" was at the birth of Lara. Obviously, there were physical as well as mystical happenings going on. But after the exhilaration of her birth, I remember sitting up on the delivery table, totally unselfconscious of my nakedness in the presence of others, and shaking uncontrollably. I had just witnessed, just taken part in the miracle of creation, of new birth!

And just perhaps, at Grandma's graveside, I was sensing anew my earthiness, my vulnerability. As generations before you die, one becomes aware of one's own mortality. I've been somewhat cushioned from that reality by having both parents and grandparents alive. Now, I feel a step closer to my own confrontation with the Divine.

Bishop Sauder followed the reading of my letter to Grandma with the appropriate readings and scriptures, as he has quoted them hundreds of times. In his ragged, black, plain coat and hat, he seemed to represent an era in the Mennonite Church that had clearly influenced the woman whose body lay inside that ugly, gray casket. The dogmatism of that era had taken a lively, outspoken, young woman with sparkling eyes and broad brimmed hat and had put her into long cape dresses, black stockings, and head coverings.

But thank God, the church was never quite able to stifle her spirit. True, as a woman, she never spoke publicly in church. But she did rule her home and motel business with outspoken clarity and authority. And when she died, she was buried in a bright, robin-egg-blue dress with an open embroidered circle at the breast—a dress she had picked out herself.

When the Bishop's "ashes to ashes and dust to dust" recitation was finished, Grandpa again interjected the somberness with a song. And then, with finality, Grandpa rather abruptly turned and said, "Amen, Amen! Let's get out of here." And with that, this trim, 93-year-old man with tan raincoat and navy blue beret, headed back to the church. Alone with his cane, he spurned the hands offered him by his daughters.

As dusk set in, I took the dried, wild flowers—my one last memory to Grandma—which I had placed on the top of her casket. I opened the lid and tucked them under the satin sheet next to her cold, hand. "Farewell, Grandma. You live on but certainly not in that body. We loved you, love you still."

Further Reading Options
A Sampling Compiled by the Editor

We are never without role models as long as books about women exist and women are literate and choose to read. When I read their biographies decades ago, Lucretia Mott, Dorothea Dix, and Antoinette Brown Blackwell became mentors for me. We might draw from Mennonite writers: Dorothy Friesen, *Critical Choices: A Journey with the Filipino People*; Frances Hiebert "Missionary Women as Models in the Cross-Cultural Context" in *Missiology*, Oct. 1982; LaVonne Godwin Platt, *Bela Banerjee: Bringing Health to India's Villages*.

Our lives could be enriched through women's personal stories: Cho Wha Soon's, *Let the Weak be Strong*; *Child of the Dark: The Diary of Carolina Maria de Jesus*; or Anne Moody's autobiography, *Coming of Age in Mississippi*. Or we might choose books because of their subtitles— *Bamboo Shoots After the Rain: Contemporary Stories by Women Writers of Taiwan*, Ann C. Carver and Sung-Sheng Yvonne Chang, editors; *Nan: The Life of an Irish Travelling Woman*, by Sharon Gmelch; *Both Right and Left Handed: Arab Women Talk about Their Lives*, by Bouthaina Shaaban.

But further resources provide useful information beyond the story form. The following listing, for varied reasons, might prompt you to expand both knowledge and sensitivity toward women's global experience.

Adams, Carol J., ed. *Ecofeminism and the Sacred*, NY:Continuum, 1994.

Albrecht, Lisa and Rose M. Brewer, eds. *Bridges of Power: Women's Multicultural Alliances*. Phila:New Society Pub., 1990.

Amanedica Collective. *Revolutionary Forgiveness: Feminist Reflections on Nicaragua*. NY:Orbis, 1987.

Carmody, Denise Lardner and John Tully Carmody. *Prayer in World Religions*. NY:Orbis, 1990.

DuBois, Ellen Carol and Vicki L. Ruiz, eds. *Unequal Sisters: A Multicultural Reader in U.S. Women's History*. NY:Routledge, 1990.

Eck, Diana L. *Encountering God: A Spiritual Journey from Bozeman to Banaras*. Boston:Beacon, 1993.

Eck, Diana L. and Devaki Jain, eds. *Speaking of Faith: Global Perspectives on Women, Religion & Social Change*. Phila:New Society Pub., 1987.

Ecumenical Decade 1988-1998: Churches in Solidarity with Women, Prayers & Poems, Songs & Stories. Geneva:WCC, 1988.

Fabella, Virginia and Mercy Amba Oduyoye, eds. *With Passion and Compassion: Third World Women Doing Theology*. NY:Orbis, 1988.

Fabella, Virginia and Sun Ai Lee Park, eds. *We Dare to Dream: Doing Theology as Asian Women*. Hong Kong:Asian Women's Resource Centre for Culture and Theology, 1989.

Hirshfield, Jane, ed. *Women in Praise of the Sacred: 43 Centuries of Spiritual Poetry by Women*. NY:HarperCollins, 1994.

Isasi-Diaz, Ada Maria and Yolanda Tarango. *Hispanic Women: Prophetic Voice in the Church*. Mnpls:Fortress Pr., 1992.

Kyung, Chung Hyun. *Struggle to be the Sun Again: Introducing Asian Women's Theology*. NY:Orbis, 1991.

Leonard, Ann. *Seeds: Supporting Women's Work in the Third World*. NY:Feminist Pr./CUNY, 1989.

May, Melanie A., ed. *Women and Church: The Challenge of Ecumenical Solidarity in an Age of Alienation*. Grand Rapids & NY:Eerdmans & Friendship, 1991.

Nyce, Dorothy Yoder. *Strength, Struggle, and Solidarity: India's Women*. Goshen:Pinchpenny Pr./Goshen College, 1989.

Oduyoye, Mercy Amba. *Who Will Roll the Stone Away? The Ecumenical Decade of the Churches in Solidarity with Women*. Geneva:WCC, 1990.

Oduyoye, Mercy Amba and Musimbi R.A. Kanyoro. *The Will to Arise: Women, Tradition, and the Church in Africa*. NY:Orbis, 1992.

O'Neill, Maura. *Women Speaking Women Listening: Women in Interreligious Dialogue*. NY:Orbis, 1990.

Peterson, V. Spike and Anne Sisson Runyan. *Global Gender Issues: Dilemmas in World Politics*. Boulder:Westview Pr., 1992.

Pobee, John S. and Barbel von Wartenberg-Potter. *New Eyes for Reading: Biblical and Theological Reflections by Women from the Third World*. Geneva:WCC, 1986.

Rao, Aruna, ed. *Women's Studies International Nairobi and Beyond*. NY: Feminist Pr./CUNY, 1991.

Russell, Letty M., Kwok Pui-lan, Ada Maria Isasi-Diaz, and Katie Geneva Cannon, eds. *Inheriting our Mothers' Gardens Feminist Theology in Third World Perspective*. Phila.:Westminster, 1988.

Seager, Joni and Ann Olson. *Women in the World An International Atlas*. NY: Simon & Schuster, 1986.

Tamez, Elsa. *Against Machismo*. Oak Park, IL:Meyer Stone Bks, 1987.

Thisthlethwaite, Susan and Mary Potter Engel, eds. *Lift Every Voice: Constructing Christian Theologies from the Underside*. NY:Harper & Row, 1990.

About the Editor

Dorothy Yoder Nyce began her sojourn to India in 1962. She lived or visited there at six different times; for four years she served on the staff of Woodstock School in the north or Kodaikanal International School in the south. *To See Each Other's Good* follows naturally from her friendship with people of diverse countries and viewpoints.

Dorothy's book, *Strength, Struggle, and Solidarity: India's Women*, resulted from observation, from reading Indian writers, and from the privilege of joining a Fulbright-funded study tour, arranged through the United States Educational Foundation in India, titled "Women, the Family, and Social Change in India." Her book content also formed the basis for lectures awarded by the C. Henry Smith Peace Lectureship for 1988-89.

Her immediate family consists of her husband, John, and adult daughters, Lynda and Gretchen. Numerous others, especially from Asia, have lived with Nyces, short-term. That 300 meals were eaten by other than immediate family at 1603 South 15th during 1995 combined both hosting interest and a husband's skills with curries. During eleven weeks of 1993, John and Dorothy had visited and experienced the gracious hospitality of families of over twenty Goshen College students, in Asia.

Global interests, biblical texts, and attention to women's experience have prompted Dorothy to bring others together before. She recently created a thirty-minute video, *Holy Respect, No Less*, to foster greater openness among people of living faiths. For that, she videotaped twenty people with experience in India. Six friends created a slide set/video of global women based on the text of Proverbs 31, titled *Women of Strength Ancient and Modern*. In 1983, she edited *Weaving Wisdom—Sermons by Mennonite Women* and a year later helped create the *Mennonite Women's Calendar*. Using the International Women's Year Themes, she edited *Which Way Women?* for Mennonite Central Committee's Task Force on Women, an organization she helped bring into being.

As a current DMin student at Western Theological Seminary in Holland, Michigan, Dorothy probes questions of Hindu-Christian exchange. She completed an MDiv from Associated Mennonite Biblical Seminaries, Elkhart, Indiana, in 1981. Since then, she has taught "Bible and Sexuality" at Goshen College, her Alma Mater. Other teaching, preaching, and writing opportunities complement her interest in research.

Broader church efforts prompt the volunteer in Dorothy. She has served several years as Worship Coordinator for the campus cluster of Assembly Mennonite Church, Goshen. For eight years a board member of the Mennonite Board of Missions, she chaired the Overseas Divisional Committee five years. She wrote about three topics and ten missionaries for *Mennonite Encyclopedia, Vol. V. Jesus' Clear Call to Justice*, her study of Luke texts, appeared in the Peace/Justice Series from Herald Press.

About the Artist

Laurel Voran, a gardener and freelance artist, was graduated from Goshen College with a degree in graphic art and natural science. She enjoys any outdoor adventure; to hike in Nepal was a highlight. With that trip, she also came to appreciate India's people and culture by volunteering with the Sisters of Charity and a Women's Development Centre in Calcutta, India, for several months of 1991.

Voran's art work has been displayed at Goshen College and at a public library in Fort Wayne, Indiana. She has also overseen the visual environment for worship in her congregation.

After working several years as a gardener at Greencroft, a large retirement community in Goshen, Indiana, Laurel is currently participating in a professional gardener training program at the world-renowned Longwood Gardens in Pennsylvania.

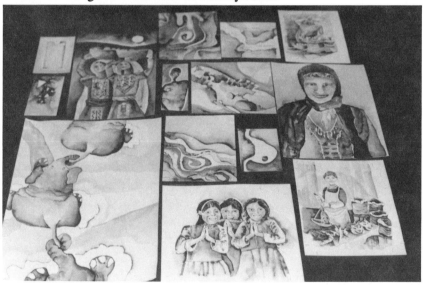

DATE DUE

MAR 2 3 1996			

GAYLORD   PRINTED IN U.S.A